STARRY SKY ADVENTURES UTAH

HIKE, PADDLE, AND EXPLORE UNDER NIGHT SKIES

Crystal White

FALCON GUIDES

GUILFORD, CONNECTICUT

FALCONGUIDES®

An imprint of Globe Pequot, the trade division of The Rowman & Littlefield Publishing Group, Inc.
4501 Forbes Blvd., Ste. 200
Lanham, MD 20706
Falcon.com

Falcon and FalconGuides are registered trademarks and Make Adventure Your Story is a trademark of The Rowman & Littlefield Publishing Group, Inc.

Distributed by NATIONAL BOOK NETWORK

Photos by Bettymaya Foott
Photo on p. 8 by Finley Holiday Productions
Photos on p. 29 by Ron Gleason
Photo on p. 47 by Ryan Andreasen
Photo on p. 54 by Louis Kamler

Maps by Melissa Baker

British Library Cataloguing in Publication Information available

Library of Congress Cataloging-in-Publication Data available

ISBN 978-1-4930-5728-3 (paper: alk. paper)
ISBN 978-1-4930-5729-0 (electronic)

∞™ The paper used in this publication meets the minimum requirements of American National Standard for Information Sciences—Permanence of Paper for Printed Library Materials, ANSI/NISO Z39.48-1992.

CONTENTS

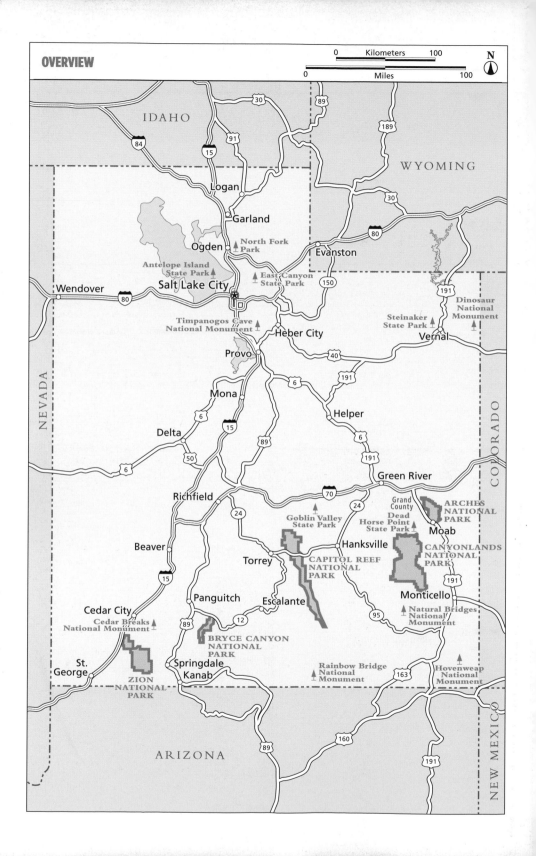

Kilometers
0   100

0   100
Miles

N

IDAHO

WYOMING

Logan

Garland

North Fork
Park

Ogden

Evanston

Antelope Island
State Park

East Canyon
State Park

Wendover

Salt Lake City

150

191

Dinosaur
National
Monument

NEVADA

Timpanogos Cave
National Monument

Heber City

Steinaker
State Park

Vernal

Provo

40

191

Mona

6

Helper

Delta

6

89

6

50

191

6

Richfield

Green River

Grand
County

ARCHES
NATIONAL
PARK

Beaver

24

24

Goblin Valley
State Park

Dead
Horse Point
State Park

Moab

Hanksville

CANYONLANDS
NATIONAL
PARK

Torrey

CAPITOL REEF
NATIONAL
PARK

191

Panguitch

Escalante

Monticello

Cedar City

Cedar Breaks
National Monument

12

95

Natural Bridges
National
Monument

BRYCE CANYON
NATIONAL
PARK

St.
George

Springdale

Kanab

Rainbow Bridge
National
Monument

163

Hovenweep
National
Monument

ZION
NATIONAL
PARK

COLORADO

ARIZONA

89

160

191

NEW MEXICO

MEET YOUR GUIDES

Author **CRYSTAL WHITE** grew up surrounded by the natural beauty of Star Valley, Wyoming. In the expansive landscape of her youth, she was drawn to watching the natural world and feeling in awe of the wonders she discovered there. An avid camper, Crystal spends many nights under a star-filled sky, fueling her curiosity of the universe. As a night sky ranger-naturalist, she was responsible for the first Utah state park being certified as an International Dark Sky Park: Dead Horse Point State Park.

Owner and lead guide of Moab Astronomy Tours, she is a Certified Interpretive Guide through the National Association for Interpretation, a professional naturalist of seventeen years, and an amateur astronomer of fourteen years. She was recently selected as a NASA Solar System Ambassador, volunteering with the Jet Propulsion Laboratory, and receives intense training from the scientists and engineers throughout NASA's network of centers. Her true passion in life lies in conserving our view of the universe and keeping the night sky clear for everyone to draw inspiration and wonderment. Crystal works with the International Dark Sky Association and the Colorado Plateau Dark Sky Cooperative and is a cofounder of Moab Dark Skies.

Photographer **BETTYMAYA FOOTT** grew up in picturesque Moab, Utah. Spending summer nights sleeping on the family trampoline under the stars, she fostered an early appreciation for the night sky. She graduated from the University of Utah Honors Program with an HBS in Environmental and Sustainability Studies and a minor in Spanish Language. Her night sky photography began when working for Utah State Parks, starting twelve International Dark Sky Park applications across the state and using photography to document the quality of the night skies. Today she leads a global team of advocates for the International Dark Sky Association as Director of Engagement. Preserving dark skies is her life goal, and she finds that astrophotography is the most poignant way to express a love for the night, as well as educate others about the impacts of light pollution. Her work has been featured in *National Geographic*, *Sky and Telescope*, the *Los Angeles Times*, and National Park Service publications. She is passionate about increasing diversity in the field of astrophotography and is proud to be working with an astronomy business run and owned by women. You can see more of her work at www.bettymayafoott.com and on Instagram at @bettymaya.foott.

INTRODUCTION

STANDING UNDERNEATH A TRULY DARK NIGHT SKY filled with stars is an experience never forgotten. The constellations get lost in the myriad pinpoints of light. Faint meteors streak across the sky on most nights, with the occasional fireballs during meteor showers. The arm of the Milky Way steeped in legend seems to have a structure to its form. For a moment, you even believe you can see purples and greens in that arm.

An hour after sunset in the spring, a stunning triangle of light shoots up from the western horizon. In the fall, an hour before sunrise, the same triangle of light shoots from the eastern horizon. This phenomenon is called zodiacal light, sunbeams lighting up dust in space from the creation of our solar system. It is a sight to behold, but only in natural darkness.

Perseus, Cassiopeia, Cepheus, Andromeda, and Pegasus travel across the winter night sky, playing out a generations-old Greek drama full of vanity, angering the gods, betrayal, heartbreak, bravery, survival, a bit of magic, and a happy ending. Hidden within these constellations, one can find star clusters, nebulae, galaxies, and more.

In the spring, Orion and his dogs take center stage. They spend the night hunting the animals across the sky with Scorpius hot on their trail. Within Orion's sword lies the Orion Nebula, a diffused nebula of hot gases and matter creating hundreds of stars. Found within Gemini is a planetary nebula called the Eskimo Nebula. A planetary nebula is the end of a small star's life. After the red giant phase, when fusion is no longer happening in the core of the star, hydrogen to helium fusion begins in the shell, and the star starts to puff out like a marshmallow over a campfire.

The birds of the sky take over in summer, with Cygnus and Aquila flying along the Milky Way and Corvus riding the back of Hydra, the snake. Vega, Altair, and Deneb form the Summer Triangle linking Cygnus, Aquila, and Lyra together. Hercules can also be sighted, taking on Draco, the dragon, as he completes one of his feats. The Veil Nebula, a large nebula that seems painted in a long stroke across a wing of Cygnus, the swan, is the remnant of a massive star's death. A high-mass star holds a core much more massive than smaller stars. During nuclear fusion, the centers are so hot and so active that when all the hydrogen turns to helium, more exotic types of fusion occur until iron is formed within the core. Iron being so heavy, the center becomes unstable as the force of gravity pushes in, and the star explodes in a brilliant supernova.

The fall is met with the zodiac constellations of Capricorn, Aquarius, Sagittarius, and Pisces. Zodiac constellations travel the same path as the sun, moon, and all the planets. As Earth turns on its axis, the constellations seem to move across our night sky from east to west. Just below the constellation Cassiopeia, our nearest galactic neighbor is visible stretching across the view in my telescope. The Andromeda Galaxy is about 2.5 million light-years away from our own Milky Way Galaxy and about twice as large with over a trillion stars. In the future of the universe, these two galaxies will merge into a new, more massive galaxy.

Most of us can remember where we were and who we were with when we first experienced a starry sky. For me, I was a young child living in Wyoming; my sister and I spent most summer nights sleeping out in hammocks or on the trampoline. Many nights, I would wake mid-night to watch the Milky Way, planets, and stars shift across the sky from east to west. I would learn later what a marvel it was to experience this as children.

I spend a lot of time talking with people about dark sky conservation. Everyone I've asked can remember their first time under a truly dark night sky. They often speak to feeling small or insignificant after learning how vast the universe is. Feeling insignificant is a curious feeling once you consider that our human origins, our elemental makeup, comes from the death of high-mass stars within that same universe. We are a collective conscious of the universe, a mirror of creation through cataclysmic explosions. We are the universe manifesting itself, as the elements created within the universe are within us.

For generations, the superstition of nightly things kept most humans indoors at night. Only nyctophiles, werewolves, witches, vampires, and chupacabras would be caught outside at night, right? This guide is designed to turn you into a lover of the night—a nyctophile! There are many adventures in this guide designed to keep you out under the stars while being active. Let your peers say you're batty, a lunatic for going out at night to recreate. Bats and the moon are pretty cool, so you'll be in excellent company.

Vincent van Gogh wrote, "For my part, I know nothing with any certainty, but the sight of the stars makes me dream." I hope this guide inspires you to seek out dark places and dream as well.

IMPORTANCE OF NATURAL DARKNESS

For millions of years, all life on Earth evolved under predictable patterns of light and dark. During the day, our star Sol lights up the Earth, giving terrestrial life the light needed to grow, reproduce, and be active. As the Sun sets, the sky is bathed in warmer colors of orange, pink, and red. This transition in light prompts life to slow down, relax, rest, and recover from a day full of activity. Light at night is left to the cycles of Earth's Moon and the planets of the solar system reflecting sunlight back toward Earth, starlight, bioluminescence, aurora, volcanic lava as it runs down the cone, and lightning during thunderstorms. Life evolved adapting to these shifts of light and dark.

These patterns of light and dark remained relatively unchanged until the last few hundred years. Light use from humans began with fires to keep warm and keep predators away. In time, man used whale oil to light lanterns along our cobblestone streets, then switched to candles. In 1879, Edison designed the commonly used lightbulb, which would change

the world in ways he never could have predicted. In the mid-1930s, the Rural Electrification Act brought outdoor light to rural communities across the United States.

The sun and moon cycles set a circadian rhythm, a wake-sleep cycle that the health of all life is bound to. At night our bodies produce a hormone called melatonin. This hormone induces sleep, a time of rest and recovery within the body. It begins the processes that result in lower blood pressure and cholesterol, cell repair, and improved immune response, staving off many unpleasant health issues.

Research has shown that even the slightest change in lux above the level of a full moon results in suppression of melatonin production for the night. In a world full of technological advances, our electronics and lights outshine the full moon, resulting in many known side effects when exposed to their light at night, such as high blood pressure; obesity; breast, colon, and prostate cancer; sleep and mood disorders; and stalling melatonin production.

Why do LED lights have such a profound effect? It is due to the blue-white light that emanates from them. Blue light moves in a very rapid wave with intense energy. This light tells our bodies it is time to rise and get active for the day. Exposure to it after dark leads to the issues mentioned above.

How do we best reduce the effects of artificial light at night? By following the lead of our planet's patterns. As the sun sets, it falls within the thick part of the atmosphere, just above the horizon. Particulates bend the light beams at this angle, scattering all but the warmer colors. This is called Rayleigh scattering, which results in beautiful orange and red sunsets. These slow waves of light bring relaxed energy. It is a signal for our bodies to

slow down and prepare for sleep. If we surround ourselves with warmer colored light at night, it sends us the same signals, resulting in more restful sleep once the lights are out.

Today, around the globe, most children cannot see the Milky Way from their urban homes. Many urban-dwelling adults simply do not even think to look up, as most of the sky is lost in the orange of skyglow. It makes me wonder what may be lost in this new reality where our nights are so bright, we forget to look up. The inspiration gained by past scientists, artists, composers, and inventors by being able to look up into the night sky led to many beautiful discoveries and works of art. What scientific discoveries, inventions, works of art, poems, and stories might never come to fruition due to being cut off from our view of the universe, our origins?

We are not the only species affected by artificial light at night. It seeps into ecosystems, affecting many species, causing another stressor on top of all the other stressors they face from climate changes and habitat loss. Bird populations are declining across the world at a staggering rate due to collisions with buildings after being temporarily blinded, amphibians are found to produce their mating call less, newborn sea turtles head inland instead of out to sea, plants are not being pollinated by the insects they rely on to reproduce—all this due to the impacts of artificial light at night. And this is only a small fraction of the ecological degradation we are finding because of our need to light up the night.

The situation might sound dire, but intelligent humans continue to innovate. Developing lighting designs can shine light downward only, and shine in the warmer Kelvin temperature range, minimizing many negative effects of light pollution and saving electricity. It is estimated that approximately 30 percent of all outdoor lighting is wasted shining directly upward into space, creating skyglow. This equates to nearly $3 billion, often sourced from nonrenewable sources of energy, money spent on lights shining into space where only astronauts can see it.

DARK SKIES

DEFINITIONS

IDA: International Dark Sky Association
A nonprofit organization with the mission to protect the night sky for this and future generations.

IDSC: International Dark Sky Community
A community certification given to communities that adopt lighting ordinances and codes to prevent light pollution and protect the health of ecosystems, as well as residents' health and safety.

IDSP: International Dark Sky Park
A park certification given to parks that adopt lighting management plans to prevent light pollution and protect the health of ecosystems, as well as visitors' health and safety.

IDSR: International Dark Sky Reserve
A certification given to areas, including various landowners, that adopt lighting management plans to prevent light pollution and protect the health of ecosystems, as well as residents' health and safety.

ALAN: Artificial light at night

BORTLE SCALE: A scale of night sky brightness that helps identify areas that are genuinely dark, untouched by light pollution, and areas where light pollution is affecting the view of the night sky. The scale moves from 1, a night sky unblemished by artificial light at night, to 9, a night sky bathed in orange glow where only the brightest stars, planets, and the moon can be seen in the night sky.

LIGHT POLLUTION: Unnecessary light that washes out the view of the universe.

SKYGLOW: The orange glow that is seen above most cities, caused by light shining in all directions and reflecting off particulates and clouds.

GLARE: Light shining at an angle that shines directly into the eyes of a person at night, walking or driving toward the light, before the person is directly underneath the light.

KELVIN: A measurement of the color temperature.

MAGNITUDE: Brightness of stars.

THREATS TO OUR VIEW OF THE NIGHT SKY

With the efficiency and brightness of LED lights, cities and rural communities across the globe are lighting up the night to the level of daylight. Often light fixtures are not shielded, and the bulbs are exposed to view. With light shining in all directions, the night sky is bathed in light of varying degrees, based on the size of the community. Lights often do not have timers, sensors, or dimming abilities.

LED technology is currently one of the most energy-efficient methods of light. It is ideal to use LED lighting to reduce energy use and the cost of that energy. LED bulbs are now being made with amber chips, which are a warmer color temperature.

By shielding all exterior lightbulbs with a fixture that directs light downward only and by placing a warmer-colored bulb (3000K or less) within the installation, skyglow could be reduced to the lights coming from internally lit billboards, significantly decreasing skyglow coming from communities. By adjusting the angle, one can even eliminate much of the glare coming from shielded fixtures, and ensure the light is directed onto the ground where it is intended to be used.

Glare can significantly affect pedestrians and drivers as they make their way through our communities. As we age, our eyes do not adapt as quickly to changes from light to dark. It takes approximately 20 minutes to adjust, a time that city drivers may not have when leaving brightly illuminated areas into rural roadway areas. Downward-facing light protects pedestrians from blindly stepping into roadways.

HOW CAN YOU PROTECT THE NIGHT SKY?

There are really just a few simple steps to help reduce light pollution in your home and communities. Starting with your own home, ask yourself these questions: Do I really need light here at night? Could the light I need be placed on a motion sensor, timer, or dimmer? Does any of my exterior lighting trespass onto my neighbors' property? Are all of my lights shielded to direct light downward only and where I need it? Am I using the most efficient bulb in a warm color temperature? Do I notice any glare coming from the light fixtures? What intensity of light is needed in this location? Making any small adjustments to your exterior lighting will help reduce light pollution. This same technique can be used for businesses, community organizations, and government agencies as well.

If you would like to take your protection efforts a step further, you could always join a local IDA chapter (www.darksky.org/our-work/grassroots-advocacy/chapters/find-a-chapter/). You could work with your community leaders to improve your city's outdoor lighting codes. You could donate money to organizations that help protect, mitigate, and educate individuals on the effects of artificial light at night. You could join a citizen science effort such as Lost at Night (www.lostatnight.org) or Globe at Night (www.globeatnight.org).

DARK SKY PLACES PROGRAM

In 1988, the International Dark Sky Association established the International Dark Sky Places program, proving itself to be a world leader in protecting natural darkness around the globe. This guide will highlight those established dark sky places, as well as a few in progress, and identify fun adventures to be had underneath their dark skies.

In 2006, Natural Bridges National Monument in Utah's San Juan County became the first International Dark Sky Park in the world, leading the way for many Utah parks and monuments to follow. But it was not until 2014 that another Utah park or monument did follow, with Hovenweep National Monument. In 2015 the program took off in Utah, with Capitol Reef National Park, Weber County's North Fork Park, and Canyonlands National Park all earning certification. The following year, Dead Horse Point State Park and Goblin Valley State Park were certified, and in 2017, Antelope Island State Park and Cedar Breaks National Monument.

During 2018, Torrey, Utah's first International Dark Sky Community was certified, as well as one state park and one monument—Steinaker State Park and Rainbow Bridge National Monument. Finally, in 2019 Bryce Canyon National Park and Dinosaur National Monument followed. I'm looking forward to seeing which parks, monuments, reserves, communities, sanctuaries, and urban spaces will be certified in the future. Communities and parks throughout the state are working on darkening their own skies, achieving new certifications and reducing overall light pollution across Utah.

ASTROPHOTOGRAPHY ESSENTIALS

BETTYMAYA FOOTT'S TIPS FOR TAKING PHOTOS AT NIGHT

- **EXPOSURE:** There are three things you need to remember when setting up your exposure—shutter speed, aperture, and ISO—known as the "exposure triangle."

- **SHUTTER SPEED:** Shutter speeds can range from 15 to 30 seconds. The focal length of your lens determines how long you can open your shutter without capturing the motion of the earth, evident in star trailing. This can be calculated by the "500 rule"—divide 500 by the focal length of your lens, and you will get the longest time in seconds that you can expose. For longer shutter speeds, you will need to use a star tracker to compensate for the rotation of the Earth (discussed below).

- **APERTURE:** Shoot with a wide aperture, f 2.8 or wider. A wider aperture is reflected by a smaller number. It's counterintuitive because it's describing the *ratio* of your lens's focal length (mm) to the size of the aperture.

- **ISO:** ISO settings for night skies range from 1600 to 6400. ISO refers to your camera's sensitivity to light. A higher ISO will give you more sensitivity to light. Higher ISO can cause increased digital noise (grain). This can be mitigated with a stacking technique (described later). Keep in mind higher ISO's will produce less noise on some cameras than others (newer camera models tend to produce less noise).

- **MY SETTINGS:** For photos like those you will see in this guide, I tend to shoot for 25 seconds with ISO 2000 to 6400 and f 1.8 to 2.8.

- **FOCUS:** Focus is one of the hardest parts of astrophotography. Autofocus will not work in dark shooting conditions; you must use manual focus. To find the correct focus, roughly preset your lens to infinity and enable live view (seeing the image on the screen of the camera). Center the brightest celestial object, or something distant and bright. Use the camera display zoom (not on your lens!) to zoom in as far as possible. Adjust your focus until the bright object you selected becomes as small as possible. A good sign that you are approaching focus is if you see dim stars appearing in the viewfinder. If you do not have live view, preset your lens to infinity, take an image, review and adjust the focus, and repeat the shot until you achieve a sharp image.

- **IMAGE TYPE:** Shoot in RAW format for optimal post-processing. Shooting in JPEG condenses the image, which gives you less information to work with when editing the file. Note that RAW files are larger than JPEGs, and you may need an external hard drive to store your files on.

EQUIPMENT

- **CAMERA:** Any DSLR (digital single lens reflex) camera will capture images of the night skies. A camera with a full frame sensor will enable the most light capture, but it is not necessary for good-quality night sky photos. Live view capabilities make focusing much easier!

- **LENS:** For landscape astrophotography, shoot on a wide-angle lens (50 to 12 mm) with a wide aperture of f 2.8 or larger (smaller number). A good all-around astrophotography lens is the Rokinon 14mm f 2.8.

    It's possible to capture images of deep sky objects like nebulae and galaxies using a zoom lens mounted on a star tracking device. You can also attach your camera body to a telescope, as long as it's tracking the motion of the earth. The best images taken of these deep sky objects are made via a stacking process to reduce noise, and also an HDR process to capture the range of exposures.

- **REMOTE RELEASE:** Anything that keeps your hand from vibrating the camera will give you sharper, higher-quality shots. Although not necessary, you can also use the 2-second timer on your camera to release the shutter without touching the body.

- **TRIPOD:** Absolutely necessary for night sky photography! As hard as you try, you won't be able to hold still for over 20 seconds. You can use natural props, like stones or fences, if you don't have a tripod, but the ease of changing the composition of your shot is greatly enhanced with a tripod.

- **INTERVALOMETER:** For more advanced shooting techniques, like time lapses or star trails, an intervalometer is essential to capture rapid-fire images one after another.

PLANNING YOUR TRIP

Now it's time to plan your adventure! Many of the International Dark Sky Places listed in this guide have a busy season in which lines are long and services are taxed. It's always a good idea to contact the nearest tourist information office for the place you plan to visit. Also, keep in mind that when it is busy, sometimes needed resources run out. Come prepared! Most parks and monuments publish details for visitors to use in planning their visit. You can always find a section on planning your trip on their website, as well as a park map. Usually the website is where you can go to secure permits as well. You will need a permit for many of the river trips, multiday four-wheel-drive trips, and backpacking trips. Many of the parks and monuments will *not* have water, food, or other services available. Be sure you have everything you need for your adventure before you arrive.

LEAVE NO TRACE SEVEN PRINCIPLES

Many of these adventures will take you into areas with fragile ecosystems. Desert ecosystems may seem void of life and desolate, but if you take the time to inspect carefully, you will see that life is all around you. Most animals in desert environments are active in the twilight or nighttime hours.

Most of the areas in this guide have biological soil crusts. The easiest way to identify this living crust is by looking for a firm soil that appears smooth like a pie crust. If you step on soil and bust through a crusty layer, you are on living soil. This soil retains moisture, fixes nitrogen, provides habitat for young seedlings, and maintains a symbiotic relationship between fungi, algae, lichens, cyanobacteria, and mosses—it is extremely fragile and vital to the future of desert life. Biological soil crust is essentially a piece of the ecosystem in its infancy, and it takes forty to one hundred years to mature (depending on moisture conditions).

The Leave No Trace Institute provides seven rules to live by in order to minimize your impact and protect the wilderness experience for others, and for the future:

1. Plan ahead and prepare.

2. Travel and camp on durable surfaces.

3. Dispose of waste responsibly, including pet waste and human waste.

4. Leave what you find.

5. Minimize campfire impacts.

6. Respect wildlife.

7. Be considerate of other visitors.

Throughout this guide, I will give you examples of how best to follow these principles for each adventure area. It is also important to know that in some areas of Utah, there are hefty fines for not collecting or properly disposing of pet and human waste. I suggest always taking wag bags (such as Restop) on any trip for human waste and dog bags for your pet. Know the rules for pets. Most areas highlighted in this guide do not allow dogs. Please respect these regulations and find a sitter or kennel for your pet. Find out more about Leave No Trace at http://lnt.org.

CULTURAL SITES PRINCIPLES

1. Do not touch archaeological site structures, cowboy camp structures, petroglyphs, or pictographs. The oils from your skin damage these ancient structures and symbols.

2. Do not take rubbings or chalk in pictographs. Take only photos home with you.

3. Leave everything exactly how you find it. Do not pile up potsherds or artifacts. Take only photos.

4. Do not enter, climb on, or lean against structures. Damage to these ancient structures happens quickly.

5. Watch children and other visitors; they may not understand these principles and would benefit from learning them from you.

6. Leave every site as you find it for future generations to enjoy.

7. These sites are essential places for the posterity of the people that left them.

LOCAL RESOURCES AND EQUIPMENT RENTALS

Supplies are listed for each adventure—make sure to plan ahead and come prepared.

The adventures in this book are accessible to a range of outdoor experience and ability levels. For some, though, the right gear can make a trip great. Check these local outfitters for gear, rentals, and local expertise.

Arrive Outdoors
http://arriveoutdoors.com
(213) 559-2482
Backcountry camping gear rentals.
Online only; contact in advance.

Back of Beyond Books
http://backofbeyondbooks.com/
artsupplies.cfm
(435) 259-5154
83 N. Main St., Moab

Regional and natural history books available as well as art supplies. Visit Back of Beyond Books to prepare for plein-air painting at Balanced Rock.

The Bike Shoppe
www.thebikeshoppe.com
(801) 476-1600
4390 Washington Blvd., Ogden
Bike and gear shop offering repair and maintenance, sales, and rentals including snowshoes and fat bikes.

Cliff Hanger Jeep Rental
http://cliffhangerjeeprental.com
(800) 562-7574
930 N. Vernal Ave., Vernal
Jeep rentals for off-roading and jeep tour adventures.

Diamond Peak Mountain Sports
www.diamondpeak.biz
(801) 745-0101
249 N. Hwy. 158, Eden
Snowshoe, cross-country ski, and fat bike rentals.

Discover Moab
www.discovermoab.com
(435) 259-8825
Central hub for information, events, and gear around Moab. Resource listings include guides, outfitters, transportation services, boat rentals, and 4x4 rentals.

Gear:30
www.gearthirty.com
(801) 732-5870
1931 S. Washington Blvd., Ogden
Locally owned gear shop offering equipment rentals including snowshoes.

Green Adventure Sports
www.greenadventuresports.com
(801) 725-8094
2097 W. 750 N., West Point
Water sports gear rentals, including SUPs, kayaks, life jackets, and paddles.

Ruby's Inn
www.rubysinn.com
(866) 866-6616
26 S. Main St., Bryce Canyon City
Hotel and venue offering activity bookings and gear rentals including Nordic skis, boots, and poles.

Thousand Lakes RV Park, Capitol Reef Jeep Rentals
http://thousandlakesrvpark.com/Jeep/JeepRentals.html
(800) 355-8995
1110 W. SR-24, Torrey
Jeep rentals available at this local RV park.

Weber State University Outdoor Program, Rental Center Winter Gear
http://weber.edu/outdoor/winter-rentals.html
(801) 626-6373
4022 Taylor Ave., Ogden
Winter gear and equipment services including cross-country ski and snowshoe rentals.

Zion Cycles
www.zioncycles.com
(435) 772-0400
868 Zion Park Blvd., Springdale
Full-service bike shop offering guided tours and bicycle rentals.

Zion Outfitter
http://zionoutfitter.com
(435) 772-5090
info@zionoutfitter.com
Equipment rentals including bicycles.

HOW TO USE THIS GUIDE

THIS GUIDE WILL SET YOU UP FOR SUCCESSFUL nighttime experiences. Adventures are arranged by region so you can find convenient experiences in northwest, northeast, southeast, south-central, and southwest Utah. Within each region, you will find areas (including national parks, towns, and specific Dark Sky Places) with adventures listed for each area. I will highlight all the need-to-know details within each activity, complete with maps, difficulty, area details, pet considerations, supplies and gear to bring along, and more.

Each activity is given an adventure experience level rating from 1 to 4:

1. I have never participated in this activity.

2. I have engaged in this activity one to five times in the past.

3. I participate in this activity often.

4. I'm an expert in this activity.

Please be honest with yourself as to your skill level when planning these adventures. Some of the adventures require prior skill for trip success. Always have a few friends or family members along for your adventures, and make sure someone else knows your plans and location. You never know what unplanned event might take place, putting you into a life-or-death situation. If you would rather go alone, take a personal location beacon along just in case you end up in an emergency situation.

CONSIDERATIONS

TIMING
Ideal times may vary for catching the moon or viewing the stars. Be sure to pay attention to the timing of each activity, as gaining the full experience may depend on it.

FEES AND PERMITS

Many sites charge admission or permit fees. Price ranges are listed for each activity and location according to the following scale:

$ = $1 to $15
$$ = $20 to $30
$$$ = over $30

Fees can change from season to season. Most parks require cash, and exact change is needed in the off-season. Call ahead or check with the park online before your visit for exact pricing.

SEASON

The prime season for each adventure is listed, helping you to have an incredible trip. It is always good to call ahead or check online to make sure conditions are as expected before you arrive.

WEATHER

The weather can be quite unpredictable throughout the year in the desert country as well as in the mountains. I suggest watching the weather forecast at least two weeks before your arrival and come prepared. You can always leave extra gear in your vehicle, but it will be a long way away if you leave it at home.

Many people die each year from exposure to heat and sunlight. The UV rays can heat your skin up quickly, and the wind can wick moisture from your skin as well. Be prepared with more water than you think you will actually need; it will save your life in an emergency. In the summertime, it is best to cover your body in a thin, long-sleeved shirt and pants to help protect your skin from sunburn, which happens fast in the desert. I've found a quick-wicking fabric works best for me. Be sure to apply sunscreen on any areas not covered in clothes.

Monsoon season kicks in about two weeks into July and ends a few weeks into September. Wicked thunderstorms can roll in quickly, and lightning in the desert often hits the ground. If you are caught in a lightning storm, find a nice patch of dirt and get as low as possible with the least amount of contact with the ground. Stay clear of rock and sand, as both are conductors, and do not stand beneath trees. Most storms pass within 30 minutes.

During winter, it is always a good idea to dress in layers. Wool is the best breathable material to wear during winter to keep you dry and warm. Bring a shell (waterproof top layer), and an extra pair of socks comes in handy.

WILDLIFE

Please respect all wildlife by staying a comfortable distance away from any animals you encounter. They will act nervous if you approach too close. If you see a defensive, flight, or alert behavior happening, you are too close. Please back away. If you respect their space, wildlife will often continue normal behaviors, giving you ample time to enjoy viewing them.

Feeding wild animals is never a good idea and against regulations. You are only passing through and will not be around to support them later. Habituated animals often do not store the necessary food caches to survive the winter. For lizards, the fat in their tails is their winter stores. If you grab a lizard and it drops its tail, its only form of defense, it may not survive the winter.

Dangerous animals you might encounter in the mountains include moose, bears, and mountain lions. If you catch sight of any of these animals, calmly return the way you came. If it is a mountain lion, do not turn your back on the animal, and make yourself look as big as possible. Groups of four or more are less likely to have an encounter.

Rattlesnakes and scorpions are the dangerous animals you may encounter while you are recreating in the desert. Sightings of either one of these species are rare. Just be sure to wear hiking boots that cover your ankle to keep you protected and look into your shoes before putting them on in the morning. Always watch where you place your hands and where you sit.

I usually bring some type of wildlife deterrent along when in the backcountry. Bear spray is the most effective; however, trying a loud noise first is always a good idea. Keep bear spray handy, as you may not have long to react.

SAFETY IN THE BACKCOUNTRY

Here are a few tips I've learned over the years on how to stay safe while recreating in the backcountry or wilderness areas of our public lands.

1. Research your planned adventure online, through maps, and by talking with the land agency that manages the area.

2. Leave a detailed itinerary with a few friends or family members. Do not deviate from your itinerary.

3. Know your route.

4. Always travel in the backcountry with a few friends. The conversations and noise will cause most large predators to run the other way.

5. Have a first-aid kit and an emergency plan. You may have to self-rescue, and you should not depend on others to save you.

6. Stay hydrated and keep your electrolytes in balance. Exposure is the number-one killer in the deserts of Utah.

7. Carry the essentials with you at all times.

   - Map and compass
   - Sun protection
   - Layers of clothing that wick away sweat or stay warm even when wet
   - First-aid kit
   - Waterproof matches
   - Food and necessary water
   - Water filtration system
   - Emergency shelter

- Knife
- Electrolyte tablets or powder
- Material for patching and repairing gear if needed
- Headlamp with extra batteries
- Wag bags for human waste and container to keep used bag in.
- Loud noisemaker or pepper spray (wildlife deterrent)
- Backpack

ASTRONOMICAL UNDERSTANDING

LUNAR CALENDAR

Each month, Earth's moon goes through a predictable pattern of the change of sunlight on its surface. We call these the phases of the moon. After a full moon, the moon will begin its waning phase, where sunlight slowly moves off the face of the moon until new moon. After new moon, the waxing phase begins, where sunlight slowly returns to the moon until full moon. The phases are crescent moon, quarter moon, gibbous moon, full moon, and new moon.

The moon is tidally locked to the Earth. This means that we will always see the same side of the moon facing Earth. The moon spins on its axis once per orbit around the Earth. As it orbits Earth, the sun will light up the side facing it. From Earth, that changes the sunlit section of the moon for us.

ECLIPTIC LINE

An imaginary line that the sun, moon, planets, and zodiac constellations follow across the sky. Here in the Northern Hemisphere, the ecliptic falls along the southern end of the night sky.

ZODIAC CONSTELLATIONS

Roman and Greek astronomers, along with many other societies, identified constellations and gave them the names of their gods, goddesses, heroes, villains, and mortals that achieved great deeds. They also relied on the stars to see their own fate. The constellations that fall on the ecliptic line are considered zodiac constellations.

ZENITH

The point directly overhead.

KEEPING YOURSELF SAFE AT NIGHT

Whenever you are planning an adventure, remember to leave details of your trip with a friend or family member not coming on the journey with you. They will need a map, details of your routes, expected timeline of the outing, and who will be going with you.

Remember to take friends with you on your adventure. It is best not to do any adventure at night solo. If you were to get injured, darkness complicates any rescue effort and

sometimes may stall rescue until daylight. With others around, you can look after each other until help comes. If it is a busy season, you may have to self-rescue. This will be extremely difficult if you are alone.

Cell service is nonexistent in most canyons, mountains, and desert areas. You may want to invest in a locator beacon depending on the risk level involved. A locator beacon will alert those you have chosen to be notified that you are okay throughout your trip at regular intervals.

Always pack a headlamp with extra batteries to provide light in case an emergency situation arises. Humans are creatures of the day, and seeing at night is not our strong suit. Pack an emergency blanket too, as temperatures in any climate may change rapidly.

MAP LEGEND

Municipal

≡(70)≡ Interstate Highway

≡(191)≡ US Highway

≡(24)≡ State Road

══════ County/Forest/Local Road

═ ═ ═ ═ Unpaved Road

├──┼──┤ Railroad

Routes

■ ■ ■ ■ ■ Featured Trail/Route

▪ ▪ ▪ ▪ Trail/Route

══════ Featured Road

═ ═ ═ ═ Featured Unpaved Road

Water Features

⬭ Lake/Large River

∿ River/Creek

Symbols

∩ Arch

≋ Boat Ramp

≍ Bridge

▲ Campground

○ City/Town

▲ Mountain/Peak

▬ Lodge

🅿 Parking

⊞ Picnic Area

■ Point of Interest

🛈 Ranger Station

🚻 Restroom

📷 Scenic View/Overlook

① Trailhead/Put-in

❓ Visitor/Information Center

Land Management

▭ National Park/Forest

▭ National Monument

▭ State/Local Park

NORTHWEST UTAH

VAST STRETCHES OF ALKALI PLAINS COVER THE MAJORITY of northwestern Utah. Salt flats stretch from the Wasatch Front to the Nevada border, bleaching the soil white. This area, named the Great Basin, is shifting westward at the rate your fingernails grow, as the Pacific Plate and North American Plate move apart.

In the belly of the Great Basin is the Great Salt Lake, a remnant of the ancient freshwater Lake Bonneville. Ancient shorelines can be seen on mountains throughout the Great Basin area. Shorelines carved by the lapping waters of this ancient lake were walked by mammoths, giant sloths, two-humped camels, two species of horses, a giant bear, extinct bison, extinct large deer, pronghorn, and many other smaller mammals that exist today. Many of those megafauna evolved into the species we have today. Pronghorn, mule deer, and bighorn sheep can be found along the rugged rises of the islands and hills.

Following the migration of megafauna, Pleistocene people first moved into present-day Utah approximately 10,000 years ago. Utah's vast marshlands and swamps attracted woolly mammoths, mastodons, saber-toothed tigers, bighorn sheep, bison, giant sloths, horses, camels, and many other animals. As the climate continued to warm and possible overharvesting occurred, much of the megafauna did not survive. The Pleistocene people migrated north to forage for fruits, seeds, nuts, roots, plants, birds, fish, and the occasional large animal.

Plants sparsely cover this vast landscape. The alkaline lovers, such as greasewood and pickleweed, can be found in plentiful numbers across the flatlands. Freshwater springs rise randomly within this area, turning brackish if not contained. An estimated 1.5 million migratory birds nest along the Great Salt Lake or within the playas and wetlands surrounding the lake. Thousands of American avocets, black-necked stilts, and eared grebes flock to the lake each spring to feed on the plentiful brine shrimp.

The lake contains many islands, most being a refuge for nesting birds. The largest island is Antelope Island, a Utah state park. This island is home to American bison, pronghorn, mule deer, and bighorn sheep. Coyotes, foxes, bobcats, and many smaller mammals live throughout the vast grasslands and rugged ridges. Ancient Precambrian rocks called gneiss cover the south end of the island, with most other stone flows consisting of ancient basalt flows or tintic quartzite.

The Wasatch Range creates the eastern border of the Great Basin. These verdant mountains provide a welcome reprieve from the heat of the valley floor during the summer months. Many rise more than 12,000 feet above sea level, with a few rising to about 14,000 feet. Aspen, Douglas fir, white pine, mountain mahogany, mountain maple, and many other trees and shrubs cover the surface. In the spring, forbs and wildflowers draw in wildlife to feed on the tender flowers.

High alpine meadows and lakes often lie just below the rocky peaks. These open meadows are popular among backpackers and a beautiful place to take in the stars on a new moon phase. The reflection of the stars can be seen on the still water surface of ponds. These meadows are also popular among elk, moose, and bears.

The peaks above are home to pikas and mountain goats. Birds of prey can often be spotted riding the thermal uplifts along the rugged ridges. On rare occasions, daring golden eagles have been known to snag a young goat off the side of a cliff for a quick meal.

The majority of residents within Utah's borders live in the Wasatch valley and foothills. Much of the light pollution is found along the corridors of the interstate and major highways along the Wasatch Front. You can often drive up one of the mountain roads to an upper parking area for stellar views of the universe.

Many of these cities were established by Mormon pioneers at the direction of their prophet, Brigham Young. Brigham brought the Mormons to the Great Salt Lake to build a life without the persecution for their beliefs they were facing in the eastern United States. They established farms along the foothills of the mountains, where spring water was easily accessed and wood for buildings easily harvested.

The first people to live in northwest Utah were the Shoshone-Bannock and Eastern Shoshone people. These nomadic people lived most of the year in family bands and joined with other families for hunting and trading. They often camped along river valleys using tepees as shelter.

Their ancestors, the Fremont, lived in caves and roamed the freshwater shores of ancient Lake Bonneville, feeding on fish, waterfowl, and plants. The Fremont people traveled much of northern Utah, leaving behind petroglyphs and pictographs on canyon walls along the way.

WEBER COUNTY'S NORTH FORK PARK

Location: 1924–1944 North Fork Park Rd., Eden, UT 84310
Dark Sky designation: 2015
Contacts: Winter: Ogden Nordic Center, (801) 399-7275; summer:

North Fork Park, (801) 399-8491, parksandrecinfo@co.weber.ut.us
Land status: County park
Maps: www.ogdennordic.com/trails-map

SET HIGHER IN ELEVATION THAN THE WASATCH FRONT, Ogden Valley is a welcome reprieve during the summer months. The valley is a naturalist's wonderland, home to many species of mountain mammals, birds, and insects. The foothills are home to many different trees, shrubs, and plants as well.

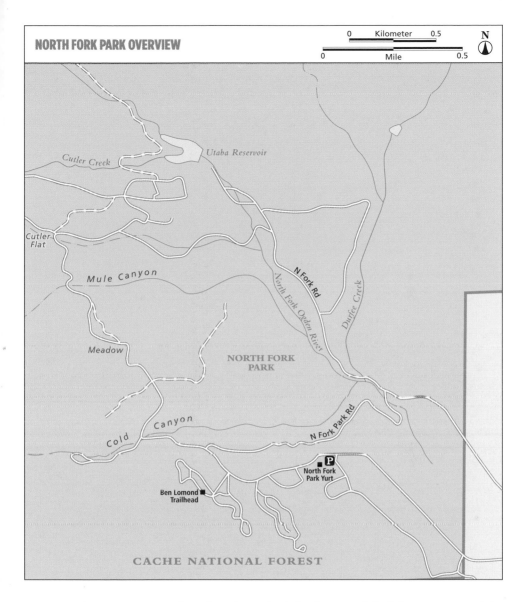

Weber County's North Fork Park is a foothills playground for hiking, mountain biking, cross-country skiing, and snowshoeing. Its varied geography offers a variety of difficulty levels for all of these sports. It is also the hub for an equestrian trail that heads up into the mountains toward Willard Peak. A variety of group campsites skirt the edge of the park.

This foothills park sees the highest precipitation in the Wasatch Front. Springtime treks up into the mountains from here present an opportunity to see many wildflowers due to increased moisture in the soil. Colors pop everywhere you look.

Enjoying the trails of North Fork Park is a year-round event. Winter and spring provide skiers, snowshoers, and fat-tire bikers a vast array of nested loops to enjoy. The Ogden Nordic Center grooms these trails for skate skiing all winter long, providing a massive playground for everyone who visits. Classic cross-country tracks are laid into the edge of the path. The flow of this trail system, with its quick uphills and gentle downhills, provides a lot of fun. With short climbs, you can often power up the hills, and long stretches of downhill provide breaks and chances to build speed. A grooming fee is required to use the trails during the winter months, and if you live close, an annual pass is available as well.

In the summer and fall, mountain biking and hiking are the primary recreational uses here. Trails lead from the valley, wind up into the wooded forest above, then return to the lowlands and wetlands. Tree cover over the trails makes shade plentiful.

Wildlife sightings are frequent in this area due to the biodiversity. Keep your eyes and ears alert, as you never know when you might come across a moose, bear, mountain lion, fox, hare, skunk, or other small mammal. With most of the larger predator animals— moose, bears, and mountain lions—if you sight one, turn around and return to where you started. Do not try to press past them. It's better to play it safe, and there are more trails in other areas.

1. SKI OR MOUNTAIN BIKE NORTH FORK PARK TO CUTLER FLATS

The groomed trails of North Fork Park are among some of the finest ski trails I have skied on. They are full of quick downhills, powerful ascents, and gentle, rolling descents for a smooth glide. The winter night sky here is incredible, with only a bit of light pollution from the Wasatch Front. Ogden Valley, the small valley in which North Fork Park rests, is an example of how a community can prevent light from shining upward, preventing wasted dollars on energy not used.

This route is also a quick night mountain bike during the winter (fat bike) and summer nights, providing all the same views of the night sky.

Activity: Nordic ski or mountain bike
Adventure rating: 2
Start: North Fork Park Nordic Center
Distance: 4.9 miles out and back
Elevation gain: 807 feet
Difficulty: Moderate to easy
Skiing time: 1.5–2 hours
Best seasons: Winter
Timing: Any time of the night
Fees and permits: $; www.ogdennordic.com/north-fork-park/trail-fees-rentals. In winter, fees will need to be paid by envelope, so bring exact cash.
Contact: North Fork Park Nordic Center, (801) 399-7275
Dog-friendly: Yes, allowed on leash (skijoring). Clean up and pack out pet (and human) waste.
Trail surface: Snow
Land status: County park
Nearest town: Eden
Other trail users: Snowshoers, horseback riders, hikers, skiers, fat-tire bikers

Maps: www.ogdennordic.com/trails-map
Special considerations: Night conditions in the winter can be brutal. Be sure you have checked the weather for storms and temperatures. Dress in layers to prevent sweat from forming. Wool clothes are the most breathable and will keep you warm even when wet. The Nordic center is closed at night.
Other: Be mindful of your surroundings. Moose encounters can be frequent, and mountain lions appear on occasion. For this trip, it is best to have a group size of 4 or more. Make your presence known.
Supplies to take: Drinking water, thermos with a warm drink, salty snacks, night sky map, Nordic trails map, smartphone with night sky app, skate or cross-country skis and poles, and headlamp with extra batteries

FINDING THE TRAILHEAD

To get to North Fork Park, I highly suggest using a GPS, as it's a rather tricky trailhead to find. From I-15 in Ogden, take 12th Street to the Ogden Canyon. Drive through Ogden Canyon until you see Pineview Dam. Turn left onto UT 158 for 4.3 miles, then turn left onto UT 162 and drive another 3 miles. Turn left onto 4100 N and travel 0.3 mile. Turn right onto 3300 E and travel 1.4 miles. At this point, you will take a left onto North Fork Road. Travel another 2 miles to the Nordic center's yurt, which should be right in front of you.

North Fork Park trailhead GPS: N41 22.483' / W111 54.150'

> Earth faces away from the galactic center in the winter, so fewer stars light up the night sky.

THE ADVENTURE

Begin skiing out the main road from the Nordic center. This section of the trail is very open, with tree line being away from the path. The trail moves through deciduous shrubs and trees before taking a hard right and dropping into Cold Canyon. This canyon is full of willows, mountain maples, conifers, and shrubs that attract wildlife.

After Cold Canyon, the trail climbs a steep pitch for about 0.25 mile. It is labeled difficult, as the steep angle may require herringbone or side steps. If your speed is good coming down, you can usually power up the pitch.

Once you're up the hill, the trail

LOOK UP

Do you see the cloudy track going through the sky next to Orion? That hazy pathway is an arm of our Milky Way Galaxy. The cloudy bit is a spiral arm of our Milky Way Galaxy filled with millions of stars, making it seem hazy.

LOOK UP

Find the constellation Orion? Once you've discovered Orion, check out his right shoulder. Can you tell that this star is the color red? Betelgeuse is a super red giant—a star that has fusion happening in its shell, which causes the star to cool and expand, puffing out like a marshmallow over a fire.

gradually slopes down with a quick power hill as you cross another small canyon. This is a beautiful spot to take in the clarity of the winter night sky.

A gradual downhill leads into Cutler Flat. Enjoy a quick downhill before making the small Cutler Flat loop, then head back up the hill and return the way you came. Cutler Flat is a great spot to take in the stars.

Returning up Mule Canyon is a bit of a haul. Once you are up this section, the main road trail seems to go by rather quickly. The most challenging part on the main road is the steep, 0.25 mile downhill back into Cold Canyon. After the climb back out of the canyon, the ski or ride is a lovely, gentle return to the yurt.

Now that you're back at your car, spend some time taking in the night sky. The winter night sky provides a crisp, clear view due to cold air not being able to hold as much moisture as warm air.

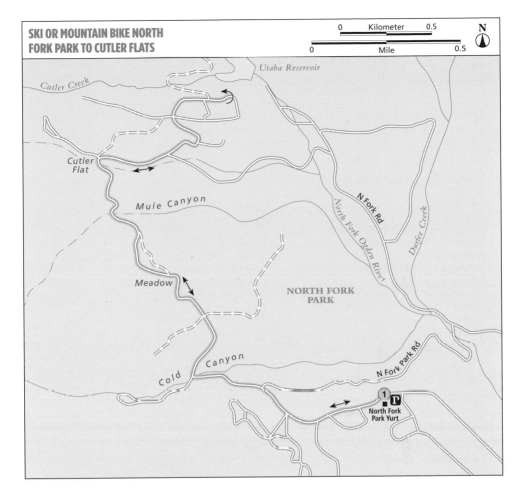

MILES AND DIRECTIONS

0.0 The North Fork Park parking area sits just east of the gate, near the yurt. Once you're ready to go, ski on the route next to the yurt.

0.38 Junction with North Fork Park Road. You will now be on North Fork Park Road for the remainder of the route.

0.71 The route dips down into Cold Canyon, followed by a steep uphill that you will need to power up.

1.2 The upper meadow provides a wide-open view of the night sky. Take a moment to check out the stars in this meadow when you return.

1.52 Mule Canyon provides a quick downhill and uphill.

1.74 Reach the edge of Cutler Flat. Enjoy the night sky while gliding along through this section.

2.45 Your turnaround point; return the way you came.

4.9 Arrive back at the parking area.

2. SNOWSHOE 365 TO PIPELINE TRAIL

This loop route will have you moving in and out of the forest, giving you snippets of the night sky from time to time. In the tree line, tracks can be found everywhere, indicating the wildlife that has already traveled by. Above tree line, the night sky will steal the show. The trail is somewhat level with gradual inclines and declines, making for an easy nighttime route.

Activity: Snowshoe
Adventure rating: 2
Start: North Fork Park Nordic Center
Distance: 2.53-mile loop
Elevation gain: 254 feet
Difficulty: Easy
Snowshoeing time: About 1 hour
Best seasons: Winter and early spring
Timing: Any time of the night
Fees and permits: $; www .ogdennordic.com/passes-rentals. In winter, fees will need to be paid by envelope, so bring exact cash.
Contact: North Fork Park Nordic Center, (801) 399-7275
Dog-friendly: Yes, allowed on leash. Clean up and pack out pet (and human) waste.
Trail surface: Snow
Land status: County park
Nearest town: Eden
Other trail users: Fat-tire bikers

Maps: www.ogdennordic.com/north-fork-park/trail-map
Special considerations: Night conditions in the winter can be brutal. Be sure you have checked the weather for storms and temperatures. Dress in layers to prevent sweat from forming. Wool clothes are the warmest and most breathable. The Nordic center is closed at night.
Other: Be mindful of your surroundings. Coming across moose at night can occur frequently, and mountain lions on occasion. For this trip, it is best to have a group size of four or more. Make your presence known.
Supplies to take: Drinking water, salty snacks, thermos with a hot drink, night sky map, Nordic trails map, smartphone with night sky app, snowshoes and poles, and headlamp with extra batteries

FINDING THE TRAILHEAD

You will be headed to the south gate of North Fork Park. To get there, I highly suggest using a GPS, as it's a rather tricky trailhead to find. From I-15 in Ogden, take 12th Street to the Ogden Canyon. Drive through Ogden Canyon until you see Pineview Dam. Turn left onto UT 158 for 4.3 miles, then turn left onto UT 162 and drive another 3 miles. Turn left onto 4100 N and travel 0.3 mile. Turn right onto 3300 E and travel 1.4 miles. At this point, you will take a slight left onto North Fork Road. Turn left and travel another 2 miles to Durfee Creek. The Nordic center's yurt should be right in front of you.

North Fork Park trailhead GPS: N41 22.483' / W111 54.150'

Moose are built for deep snow; have you ever noticed how long their legs are? They are post-holing machines. If you come across a moose, please turn around and go back the way you came.

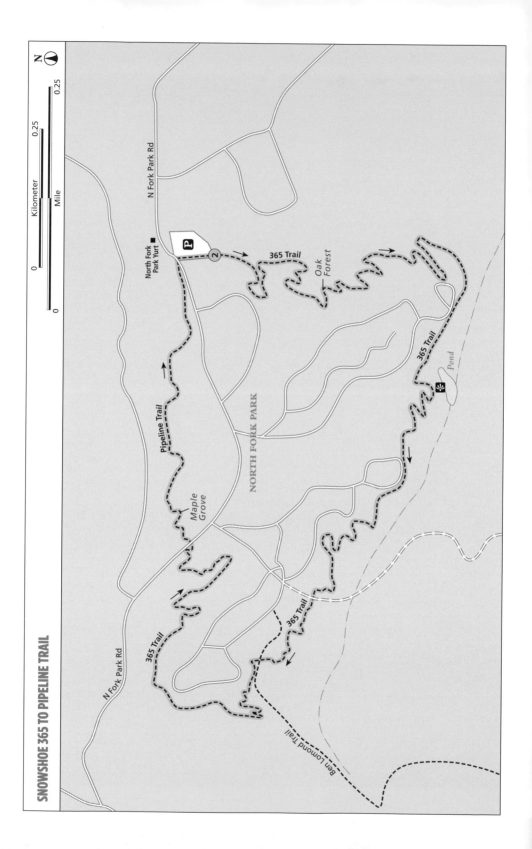

SNOWSHOE 365 TO PIPELINE TRAIL

N Fork Park Rd

North Fork
Park Yurt

P

2

365 Trail

Oak
Forest

Pipeline Trail

Maple
Grove

NORTH FORK PARK

365 Trail

365 Trail

Pond

365 Trail

N Fork Park Rd

Ben Lomond Trail

Kilometer
0   0.25

Mile
0   0.25

N

THE ADVENTURE

You'll begin this snowshoe just southwest of the main parking lot. The 365 Trail will duck into some wooded areas and skirt the open campgrounds, moving in and out of tree line. Being in the tree line will allow you to find loads of wildlife tracks. See how many you can identify as you move along this trail.

After you have reached the halfway point, the trail will move out of the tree line. Take a few minutes to enjoy viewing the night sky.

From here the trail will twist and turn in and out of the conifers and shrubs back to the yurt.

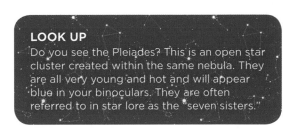

LOOK UP
Do you see the Pleiades? This is an open star cluster created within the same nebula. They are all very young and hot and will appear blue in your binoculars. They are often referred to in star lore as the "seven sisters."

MILES AND DIRECTIONS

0.0 Start at the southwest corner of the North Fork Park parking area.

0.36 The trail begins moving in and out of oak trees.

0.92 View of a pond and the mountainside. On a moonlit night, you will see them both.

1.51 Ben Lomond Trail junction; continue forward. At this location, the sky is open to view.

2.13 Groomed trail junction with North Fork Park Road.

2.19 Trail junction with Pipeline Trail.

2.53 Enjoy the gradual downhill to arrive back at the North Fork Park yurt.

Other Opportunities to Enjoy the Night Sky
NORTH FORK PARK EVENTS: MOONLIGHT GLIDE
Ogden Nordic Center holds a moonlight glide ski night around the Saturday closest to the full moon. This is a brilliant opportunity to meet nyctophiles and enjoy an evening ski with many others. The glide is from 6 p.m. to 9 p.m. For more information, contact the Ogden Nordic Center during their regular hours at (801) 648-9020. You will need to purchase a Nordic pass for this event.

ANTELOPE ISLAND STATE PARK

Location: 4528 W. 1700 S., Syracuse, UT 84075
Cost: $-$$
Dark Sky designation: 2017
Contact: Antelope Island State Park visitor center, (801) 725-9263

Land status: State park
Maps: https://stateparks.utah .gov/wp-content/uploads/ sites/13/2019/07/Brochure-Map.2019. png

THE LARGEST ISLAND WITHIN THE GREAT SALT LAKE, Antelope Island is covered with lower grasslands and a mountain range rising from the middle like a spine. The most towering peak, Frary Peak, rises from lake level at around 4,200 feet to a staggering 6,500 feet. Much of the island is covered in rugged basalt fields and metamorphic gneiss pushed up to the surface from the depths below. Jagged tintic quartzite boulders rest throughout the grasslands, and young tufa can be found close to the shorelines. The beaches are made of oolites—tiny, round marbles of mineral grains surrounded by layers of calcium carbonate.

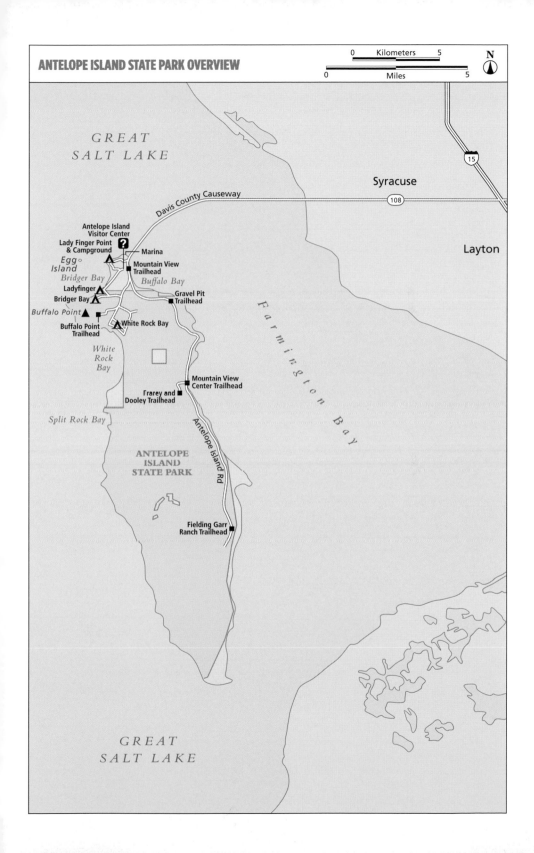

The island was prehistorically used by the Fremont people as hunting grounds. Discarded tools of these hunting parties have been found. The island's freshwater springs were used by these parties for drinking water during the hunts. The springs near Garr Ranch show evidence of being used consistently for the past 1,000 years.

In the mid–1800s, John C. Frémont was charged with surveying the lake for the US government. During his party's visit, they hunted the pronghorn on the island for meat to feed the crew. The island was named Antelope Island—believing pronghorn were a type of antelope—in honor of the meat harvested.

Icons of the American West, American bison still roam Antelope Island to this day. They range from the low grassy meadows to the high mountains that form the spine of the island. The island is also home to bighorn sheep and mule deer herds. The bighorn sheep tend to keep to the high country, close to rocky terrain for escape from predators. Mule deer can be found feeding and lounging near one of the many springs where tree cover is available. Pronghorn wander the low grasslands.

Around 1870, Fielding Garr was sent to the island to establish a ranch and care for the Mormon Church's tithing animals on the island. The Garr Ranch is the oldest building in Utah, still resting on the original foundation. Later, John Dooly would take over the Garr Ranch and turn it into one of the most extensive cattle operations in Utah. John Dooly is also responsible for moving bison to Antelope Island at a time when less than 1,000 bison existed throughout the United States.

Today Antelope Island is a haven for horseback riders, mountain bikers, hikers, wildlife viewers, and photographers. The island provides incredible vistas of the Great Salt Lake, with breathtaking mirror images when the lake is calm.

GETTING THERE

Take I-15 north of Salt Lake City to exit 332, Antelope Drive, in Layton. Follow Antelope Drive all the way to the entrance station for the park. You will drive across a 7-mile-long causeway to the island. The closest services are in Syracuse, approximately 2 miles shy of the park entrance station.

3. **NIGHT HIKE ON BUFFALO POINT**

Buffalo Point is a quick trail up to a high point with a great view of the Great Salt Lake. At the top of the point, there are several large rocks you can lie on to watch the stars. Often, when the water is still, you can see the moonlight play off the gentle ripples. It is not uncommon to come across a few bison bulls grazing on the hillside next to the trail, giving you a chance to see these amazing mammals. Don't forget to give them space. If you see a tail go up and flip back and forth, you are too close and about to be charged. Back away and give them more space.

Activity: Night hike
Adventure rating: 1
Start: Buffalo Point trailhead
Distance: 1.0 mile out and back
Elevation gain: 226 feet
Difficulty: Moderate due to incline
Hiking time: About 45 minutes
Best seasons: Summer and fall
Timing: 2–3 days after the full moon
Fees and permits: Day use, $; overnight use, $$–$$$
Trail contacts: Antelope Island State Park, 4528 W. 1700 S., Syracuse, UT 84075, (801) 725-9263, https://stateparks.utah.gov/parks/antelope-island/
Dog-friendly: Yes, allowed on leash. Clean up and pack out pet waste.
Trail surface: Dirt
Land status: State park

Nearest town: Syracuse
Other trail users: Mountain bikers, horse riders
Maps: https://stateparks.utah .gov/wp-content/uploads/ sites/13/2019/07/Brochure-Map.2019 .png
Water availability: At the visitor center before 5 p.m.
Special considerations: Be mindful of your surroundings; sometimes bison will hang out along this trail.
Other: Avoid springtime, as biting gnats hatch then and are vicious.
Supplies to take: Drinking water, salty snacks, headlamp with extra batteries, night sky map or smartphone with night sky app, binoculars

FINDING THE TRAILHEAD

Once you are on the island, follow the signs for Buffalo Point. The road follows the east side of the island then cuts across the north side, heading toward the point. The road winds through a few tight corners, then arrives at the parking area on Buffalo Point. A beautiful wooden deck with picnic tables is located just off the parking lot. Bathrooms are found at the trailhead along with a trail sign for orientation, just off the northwest end of the parking lot.
Buffalo Point trailhead GPS: N41 01.960' / W112 15.667'

THE ADVENTURE

To see both stars and moonrise, plan this hike for two to three days after the full moon. The moon rises later each night after the complete moon phase. This later rise will give you time to see the stars for a while before they are washed out by the light of the nearly full moon.

> Did you know that planets reflect sunlight, like Luna, Earth's moon? That's why they seem to shine. Starlight is created by nuclear fusion within the core of a star.

As you start up the trail, several social trails branch off to the right and a few to the left. Keep going straight up to stay on the main path. The main trail is wide from heavy use and well trodden, so it's hard to miss. Along the way, there are several benches to pause and take in the view.

As you approach the top of the hill, the trail splits; stay to the left to stay on the main path. The right branch will eventually come back to the main trail as well. After these trails merge, a single trail will take you to the boulders at the top of Buffalo Point. This is the end of the adventure and your stargazing, moonrise observation spot. Find a boulder to relax on and enjoy the evening views both of the lake and the night sky.

LOOK UP

On the night sky map, you will notice a few brighter deep space objects. Use your binoculars to look for the Andromeda Galaxy, Hercules globular cluster, and the Beehive open star cluster. Orient using the constellations to determine their location. Look for the stars Deneb, Vega, and Altair. These three stars make up the Summer Triangle (which is actually visible late spring, summer, and early fall).

Once you are relaxed and looking up, see just how many constellations you can identify before pulling out your night sky map or app. See if you can locate any planets in the night sky.

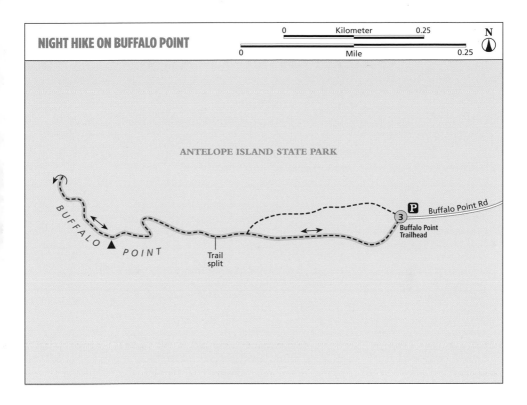

MILES AND DIRECTIONS

0.0   Start at the Buffalo Point trailhead and hike up the rise straight ahead. Take the wider of the two trails for this first section.

0.27 At this point a trail will go straight ahead but has been blocked off. Take the trail to the right, which will wind through rabbitbrush and tintic quartzite before it climbs to the next plateau.

0.36 From here it is a nice gentle incline to the top.

0.5   Turn around and head back the way you came.

1.0   Arrive back at the trailhead.

4. NIGHT SWIM IN GREAT SALT LAKE

The Great Salt Lake's water is so saline that it will push your body mostly out of the water. It's nearly impossible to swim, but also nearly impossible to sink. Effortless floating offers serenity that can only be improved by starry skies. On a warm summer night, it is quite the experience to float on your back while stargazing.

Activity: Night swim
Adventure rating: 2
Start: Bridger Bay Beach parking lot
Distance: 1.0 mile out and back (distance varies with lake level)
Difficulty: Easy
Hiking time: About 1 hour
Best seasons: Summer
Timing: 2 days before the full moon or on the full moon; about 1 hour after sunset
Fees and permits: Day use, $; camping, $$ individual and $$$ group
Contact: Antelope Island State Park, 4528 W. 1700 S., Syracuse, UT 84075, (801) 725-9263, https://stateparks.utah.gov/parks/antelope-island/
Dog-friendly: No
Trail surface: Sand
Land status: State park
Nearest town: Syracuse

Other trail users: Hikers
Maps: https://stateparks.utah.gov/wp-content/uploads/sites/13/2019/07/Brochure-Map.2019.png
Water availability: At the visitor center before 5 p.m.
Special considerations: Avoid springtime, as biting gnats hatch then and are vicious.
Other: Be sure to keep your vehicle out of the sand. Oolitic sand is like driving on marbles. You will sink deeper and deeper and move nowhere at all. A rinsing shower is in the Bridger Bay Beach parking lot.
Supplies to take: Towel, shoes or sandals, drinking water, salty snacks, and a change of clothes; you may want goggles to keep the salt water out of your eyes. Make sure goggles are not tinted, which impairs vision in the dark.

FINDING THE TRAILHEAD
From I-15 in Layton, take exit for UT 108 (Antelope Drive). Follow Antelope Drive west for 13.6 miles. Once you are off the causeway and onto the island, turn right and follow Antelope Island Road for 1.6 miles to Bridger Bay Beach parking area. The Buffalo Grill will be in the parking lot with the metal ramp.
Bridger Bay Beach parking GPS: N41 02.860' / W112 15.033'

THE ADVENTURE
From the parking area, you will find restrooms where you can change into your swimwear. The bathrooms also have an outdoor shower on the beach side to rinse off after your dip.

When you are ready, head down the beach to the lake. It is about 0.5 mile, typically with a few patches of deep sand along the way. Once you near the shore, you will be on sand that is saturated with salt water, making it firm and easy to move across. You may encounter many small flies. Brine flies are harmless to you and an excellent food source for migratory birds.

Now your adventure truly begins. If you've never swum in the Great Salt Lake, you are in for a treat. Walk out until the water is up to your waist, then just lean back and let the saline water sweep you off your feet. Floating on your back will afford you a beautiful view of the stars above.

If you want a real challenge, see if you can swim. For most people, the buoyancy makes it nearly impossible to stay low enough in the water to swim. You may want to wear goggles for this experiment.

> If you've ever bought sea monkeys on the internet, you have bought brine shrimp.

The most exciting part of swimming in the Great Salt Lake is exploring the life found in the lake. The lake is teeming with brine shrimp, a small crustacean that thrives in super-saline environments. This species is crucial to the many shorebirds that stop at the lake to refuel during migration. They also depend on the plentiful shrimp to feed their young as they nest along the lake. It is a delightful protein snack, giving them the stamina to continue on their journey as they cross the United States.

After your swim, be sure to rinse off. The salt from the lake will crystalize on your skin, causing you to itch terribly.

LOOK UP
Do you notice a difference in colors? A star's color will give you a general idea of where it is in its life cycle. Blue and white stars are young. Yellow and orange stars are middle-aged. Red stars are old stars at the end of their life.

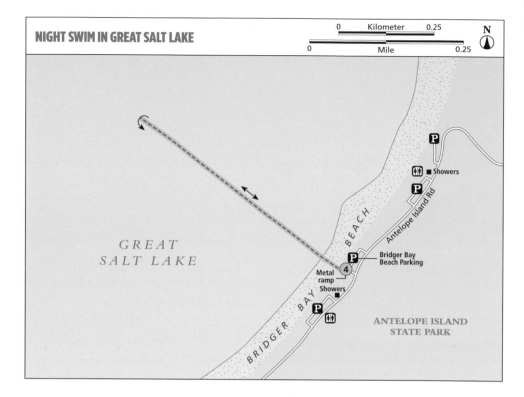

MILES AND DIRECTIONS

0.0 From the parking area, hike down the metal ramp to avoid a section of deep sand and speed up your travel.

0.13 The metal ramp ends, and a section of sand filled with sharp rocks will take you to the water or a line of vegetation.

0.3 Walk through a bit more sand onto the water-soaked beach and into the water.

0.5 This was the water level in the fall. Enjoy your float and then retrace your steps up the beach.

1.0 Arrive back at the parking area.

5. SUNSET PADDLE TO EGG ISLAND

There is nothing quite like paddling on the Great Salt Lake. When the lake is still, a mirror reflection of the clouds and landscape makes you feel like you're in a funhouse. At sunset, the red, orange, pink, and purple sunset clouds reflect on the dark gray water's surface. At night, the lights from the Wasatch Front look like dancing pencils of light across the lake's surface.

Activity: Paddle
Adventure rating: 3–4
Put-in/takeout: Marina ramp
Distance: 3.0 miles out and back
Difficulty: Moderate due to the nature of salt water and the occasional boat wake
Paddling time: 2–3 hours
Best seasons: Summer, when there is likely no wind
Timing: Plan to be on the water about 1 hour before sunset.
Waterway type: Saltwater lake
Current: Slight current in areas
Boats used: Kayaks, canoes, SUPs
Fees and permits: Day use, $
Contact: Antelope Island State Park, 4528 W. 1700 S. Syracuse, UT 84075, (801) 725-9263, https://stateparks .utah.gov/parks/antelope-island/
Land status: State park
Nearest town: Syracuse
Other lake users: Sailboats, motorboats
Maps: https://stateparks.utah .gov/wp-content/uploads/sites/ 13/2019/07/Brochure-Map.2019.png

Water availability: At the visitor center before 5 p.m.
Special considerations: Avoid springtime, as biting gnats hatch then. Egg Island is a protected island. You are not allowed to land on the island for any reason. Be cautious in your paddling. When you get salt water in your lungs, it draws water from other parts of your body to your lungs, making you asphyxiate. This is not a tour to goof around on.
Other: If winds over 10 mph are predicted, do not go out on the lake. Due to the salt content, the waves are much heavier and really slap into the boat. If you find yourself out on the lake and the wind creates intense waves, head straight to shore and pull your boat out of the water. It is a pretty quick walk back to the marina.
Supplies to take: Sea kayak, life jacket, drinking water, salty snacks, first-aid kit, headlamp with extra batteries, paddle, binoculars, and dry bag for keys and camera

FINDING THE PUT-IN/TAKEOUT

After you cross the causeway onto the island, the first area visible will be the marina. This is your put-in and takeout. A small area just off the north dock provides the best access point for sea kayaks.
Antelope Island boat ramp GPS: N41 03.700' / W112 14.390'

Brine shrimp eggs were taken into space aboard the space shuttle *Atlantis* in 1991 and hatched while in orbit. Five shrimp were still alive once they landed back on Earth. Researchers believe those that died did so from a lack of oxygen in the container. This experiment made brine shrimp the first species that we know of that was born in space.

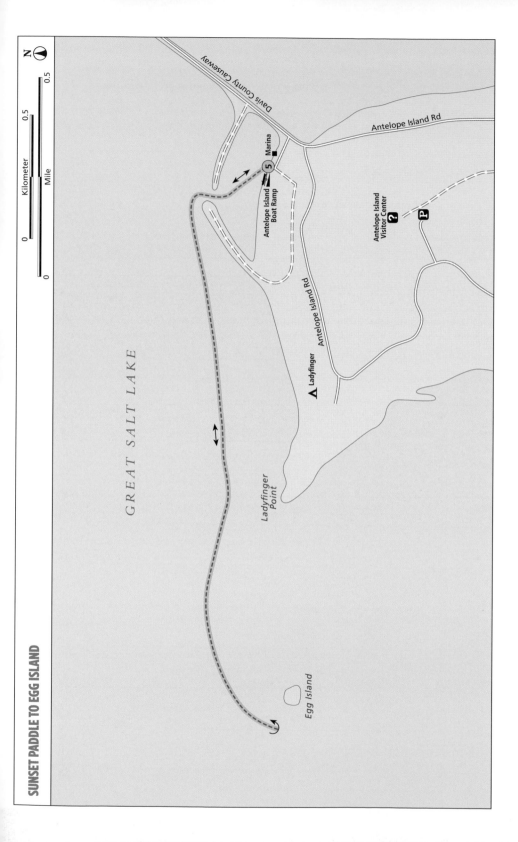

SUNSET PADDLE TO EGG ISLAND

N

0   0.5   Kilometer   0.5
0   Mile   0.5

GREAT SALT LAKE

Egg Island

Ladyfinger Point

Davis County Causeway

Marina

5

Antelope Island Boat Ramp

▲ Ladyfinger

Antelope Island Rd

Antelope Island Rd

Antelope Island Visitor Center

?

P

To the north of your location, you will notice another island; this is Fremont Island. The island is privately owned, and access is by permission only. It is home to another herd of bison and many nesting birds. To the north of Fremont Island are the higher mountains of Promontory Point. This is also privately owned, and permission is required to access it. There is a dirt road along the east side of the point to provide public access to the western desert.

THE ADVENTURE

Load up and paddle out! After exiting the marina, head northwest just off the island's shore. Follow the shoreline west from the marina until you can see Egg Island.

Once you have the island in your sight, be sure to stay on the lake side of the island, as there is a shallow sandbar on the Antelope Island side. It is fun to paddle near the island and see all the different species of migratory birds that use this island for nesting. See how many different species you can count.

This is also an excellent time to scoop a handful of water to take a closer look at the brine shrimp. They are quite unique looking and a crucial food source for many birds in this area. When you are finished, just pour them back into the lake.

LOOK UP

Looking south from here, you can identify several bright objects above the horizon in a gentle arch. The brightest objects along this arch, which astronomers refer to as the ecliptic, are planets. The ecliptic line moves through the zodiac constellation. When trying to find a planet, they will often refer to the zodiac constellation where the planet currently resides, making it easy to figure out which planet it is.

Paddling next to Egg Island, you witness this sanctuary for nesting cormorants, great blue herons, and great egrets. Many of the islands within Great Salt Lake are nesting sites for several species of birds. These islands are not to be disturbed or landed on. Often, the nests are difficult to spot, leading to unintentionally stepping on the eggs.

After the sun has set, start paddling back to make the most of the daylight you have. You should arrive back at the marina as the planets and first stars begin showing. If you'd prefer to stargaze from the water, the protection of the marina is an excellent spot for this.

MILES AND DIRECTIONS

0.0 Launch your boat from the main marina ramp.

0.2 Exit the marina area. Turn left and head west, staying somewhat close to the island's shore.

0.9 On your left, Ladyfinger Point is the closest shore to you. Straight ahead is Egg Island.

1.2 Make sure to stay on the northwest side of Egg Island. The east side of the island has a shallow sandbar connecting the two islands.

LOOK UP

On your return paddle, the planets and stars begin to shine above. The majority of what you can see above is within our galaxy, the Milky Way.

1.5 After you've reached the south side of Egg Island, head back the way you came.

3.0 Back at the boat ramp, if it is not too cold, float within the marina and watch the stars emerge.

Other Opportunities to Enjoy the Night Sky
PARK RANGER–LED EVENTS
Activity: Stargazing and telescope viewing
March through October (except July), the Ogden Astronomical Society holds a monthly star party in White Rock Bay. This event usually brings from seven to fifteen telescopes and astronomers to operate them. The night begins with an astronomy talk and ends with hours of telescope viewing. The society owns a large Dobsonian telescope named BOB (Big Ogden Bucket). For the schedule of these star parties, check out the park's event page at https://stateparks.utah.gov/parks/antelope-island/park-programs-and-events.

Great Salt Lake Bird Festival/Owling at Garr Ranch
Activity: Bird-watching
In early May, Davis County holds its annual Great Salt Lake Bird Festival. As part of the festival, there is an owling tour of Antelope Island State Park. This yearly festival is an excellent opportunity to be at the Garr Ranch long after closing time, which is prohibited otherwise. To sign up for the festival, visit www.daviscountyutah.gov/greatsaltlakebirdfest. You must register online for the tours, which fill up fast, so sign up early!

   On your way down to the Garr Ranch, you will stop to view burrowing owls and possibly even sight a short-eared owl along the way. While you are at the ranch looking for great horned owls and long-eared owls, don't forget to look up at the beautiful stars above.

Antelope by Moonlight
Activity: Bicycling
Davis County also holds an annual Antelope by Moonlight bike ride in the park. This event typically draws a large crowd of cyclists dressed up in costume for the fun ride. The ride travels from White Rock Bay to the Garr Ranch and back. This is another opportunity to enjoy the island at night without camping. Sign up at www.daviscountyutah.gov/moonlight. This ride is popular, so sign up early to participate.

EAST CANYON STATE PARK

Location: 5535 S. Hwy. 66, Morgan, UT 84050
Cost: $
Dark Sky designation: 2020

Contact: (801) 829-6866
Land status: State park
Maps: https://stateparks.utah.gov/ parks/east-canyon/directions/

EAST CANYON RESERVOIR IS A SMALL STATE PARK nestled in the Wasatch Mountains. A popular destination for boating, fishing, and camping, the East Canyon area is also steeped in pioneer history. From the Donner-Reed Party in 1846 to the many pioneer parties after, many families traveled through the surrounding area, including Mormons on their path from Illinois to Salt Lake City.

Under the full moon, the lake shimmers like a white ribbon stretched out across the water, dancing in the wind. During the early spring, many waterfowl visit the lake as part

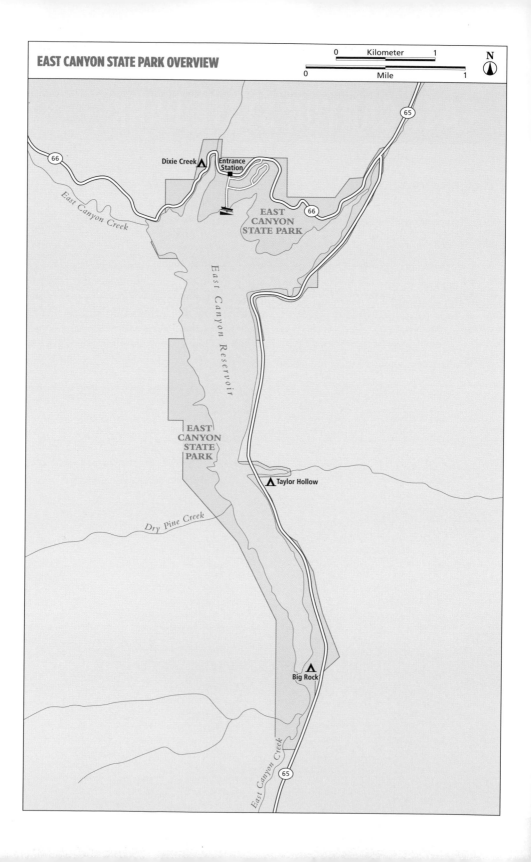

of their annual migrations. Greater sage-grouse may be found in the sagebrush steppe surrounding the lake. Black-tailed mule deer hop down for the occasional drink and browse.

With ample accommodations available, a stay at the lake is sure to reset your circadian rhythms and reduce your blood pressure. Be sure to get out at night and enjoy the sky protected by this International Dark Sky Park.

6. COMMON LOON BY FULL MOON

The lonely call of a common loon coming out of the darkness is a sound you will not soon forget. This red-eyed, black-and-white waterfowl is beautiful to see and hear. There is nothing quite like watching the moonlight glide across the water, with a common loon pair swimming into the dance while giving their yodeling call.

Activity: Night bird-watching
Adventure rating: 1
Start: East Canyon Beach
Distance: None
Difficulty: Easy
Time: About 1 hour
Best seasons: Early spring or late fall
Timing: 2 days before the full moon or on the full moon; about 1 hour after sunset
Fees and permits: $
Contact: East Canyon State Park, 5535 S. Hwy. 66, Morgan, UT 84050, (801) 829-6866, https://stateparks .utah.gov/parks/east-canyon/
Dog-friendly: No
Trail surface: Sand

Land status: State park
Nearest town: Morgan
Other park users: Campers
Maps: https://stateparks.utah.gov/ parks/east-canyon/directions/
Water availability: At the marina before 5 p.m.
Special considerations: If it is cloudy, you may not hear or see any common loons.
Other: Be sure to stay on the beach where is there is a clear view of the reservoir.
Supplies to take: Chair, spotting scope or binoculars, and warm blanket

FINDING THE BEACH

From Ogden get onto I-15 headed south for 4 miles to the connection for I-84 east. Follow I-84 east for 24.9 miles to exit 103 onto UT 66. Follow UT 66 for 15.8 miles to the park entrance. From the entrance gate, follow the park signs to the parking lot and boat ramp.
East Canyon Beach GPS: N40 55.309' / W111 35.485'

> Each male loon has a unique mating yodel. If he moves his territory, he will change his yodel to remain unique.

THE ADVENTURE

Near the picnic tables, you will see the beach ahead. Set up your spotting scope and chair, and sit back to enjoy one of the most beautiful sounds and scenes you will ever experience.

Loons are agile swimmers, diving deep to gather fish to feed on. They are also incredibly fast in the air, with rapid wingbeats. To take flight, they will run across the surface of the water for over 30 yards, an amazing sight to see by the light of the moon.

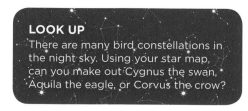

LOOK UP
There are many bird constellations in the night sky. Using your star map, can you make out Cygnus the swan, Aquila the eagle, or Corvus the crow?

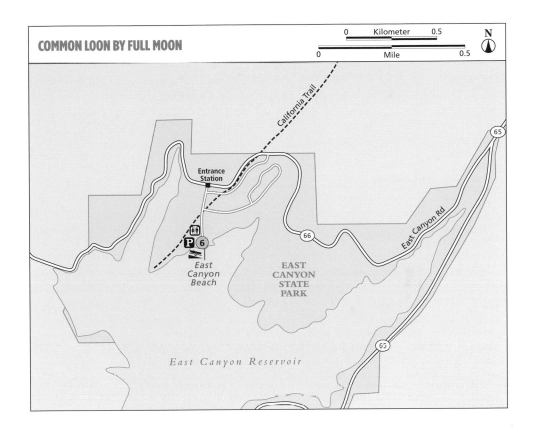

0   Kilometer   0.5

0   Mile   0.5

N

California Trail

Entrance Station

East Canyon Rd

65

66

P 6

East Canyon Beach

EAST CANYON STATE PARK

65

East Canyon Reservoir

Other Opportunities to Enjoy the Night Sky

PARK RANGER–LED EVENTS

During spring, summer, and fall, the park offers star parties. These evening events highlight the night sky found within the park and offer the opportunity to look through a telescope at deep space objects such as nebulae, galaxies, star clusters, and more. For more information on the timing of these events, visit https://stateparks.utah.gov/parks/east-canyon/events.

TIMPANOGOS CAVE NATIONAL MONUMENT

Location: 2038 W. Alpine Loop Rd., American Fork, UT 84003
Cost: Free
Dark Sky designation: 2020

Contact: Timpanogos visitor center, (801) 756-5239
Land status: National monument
Maps: www.nps.gov/tica/planyourvisit/maps.htm

Timpanogos Cave National Monument was set aside to protect the natural features within the cave system for the enjoyment of current and future generations. A steep 1.5-mile-long trail leads to the opening of the main cave. Within the cave, you will see massive stalactites and stalagmites. It is quite something to be deep within a cave, exploring the otherworldly features, and then experience true darkness when the lights are turned off. Most of the monument's night sky programs are held nearby on USDA Forest Service land in American Fork Canyon. For more information on program schedules and locations, contact the Timpanogos visitor center.

Other Opportunities to Enjoy the Night Sky
PARK RANGER–LED EVENTS
During spring, summer, and fall, the park offers star parties. These evening events highlight the night sky found within the park and offer the opportunity to look through a telescope at deep space objects such as nebulae, galaxies, star clusters, and more. For more information on the timing of these events, visit www.nps.gov/tica/planyourvisit/calendar.htm.

NORTHEAST UTAH

NORTHEASTERN UTAH IS THE LAND OF DINOSAURS and shale beds. Driving through the region, you'll notice many oil well derricks moving back and forth. The ground is full of fossil fuels from the ancient life-forms that inhabited this area. Near Vernal seems to be the hot spot of oil extraction and dinosaur fossils.

About 150 million years ago, during the Jurassic period, ten different species of dinosaurs called this area home. Their fossils have since been uncovered within the area. Over 500 different individuals have been found within the ancient river sediments of the Morrison Formation. Today, in Dinosaur National Monument, you can see these fossilized bones still in the rock within the quarry site.

The High Uinta Mountains run along the northern border of eastern Utah. These high alpine mountains host a variety of wildlife. The mountains are popular for mountain climbing, fishing, hiking, backpacking, horse-packing, and hunting. The high alpine lakes create mirror images of the pristine mountains near them. These are the ancestral lands of the Núu-agha-tʉvʉ-pʉ (Ute) people.

The valleys below are used mostly for ranching and farming. The soils are rich and fertile. The canyons are mined for coal, vanadium, uranium, and phosphates. Utah is second in the extraction of vanadium, a metal that is used as a steel additive to prevent oxidation and corrosion. The state is third in uranium extraction. This radioactive element is used in nuclear power plants and nuclear weapons.

Pronghorn are often found wandering the flatlands within this area. Desert bighorn scale the lower mountains and rocky canyons where they are sheltered from view. The high mountains are home to Rocky Mountain goats, pikas, black bears, elk, deer, mountain lions, and more. The rivers are full of native species of fish, while the lakes are often stocked with sport fish. The high alpine lakes are full of native trout species, rewarding those that hike long distances to these pristine lakes to fish.

DINOSAUR NATIONAL MONUMENT

Location: 4545 Hwy. 40, Dinosaur, CO 81610
Cost: $$
Dark Sky designation: 2019

Contact: Dinosaur National Monument visitor center, (435) 781-7700
Land status: National monument
Maps: www.nps.gov/dino/planyourvisit/maps.htm

DINOSAUR NATIONAL MONUMENT IS HOME to some of the most impressive Fremont people's pictographs and petroglyphs I have ever seen. From lizards that are over 6 feet long and 20 feet off the ground to the characteristic trapezoidal figures the Fremont are known for, they are found throughout the monument. One of the adventures here will take you to a popular panel, the Swelter Shelter. Today, these are the ancestral lands of the Núu-agha-tʉvʉ-pʉ (Ute) people.

Approximately 500 individual dinosaurs have been recorded within the monument, representing ten species of dinosaurs. Among the species found here are the carnivorous

DINOSAUR NATIONAL MONUMENT OVERVIEW

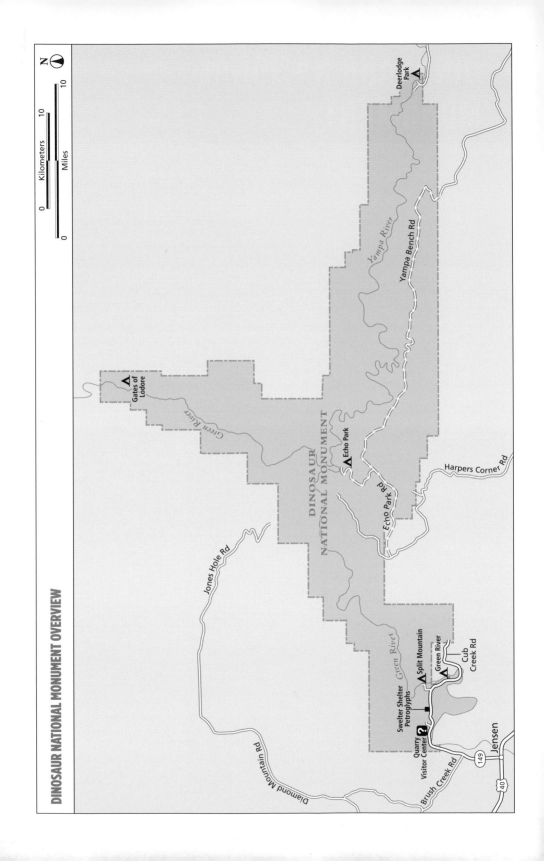

allosaurus, the long-necked diplodocus, the flying pterosaur, and the shielded stegosaurus. During the day, you can view the quarry's impressive collection of dinosaur bones still within the rock. For the dinosaur lover, this is definitely worth a visit.

The Green and Yampa Rivers have carved deep canyons, allowing the adventurer to travel back in time through the exposed layers. Whitewater rafting from the Gates of Lodore to the Utah side of the monument provides a world-class experience for boaters. There are many hikes throughout Dinosaur National Monument, most to petroglyph or pictograph panels. Remote backcountry campsites can be accessed by four-wheel-drive vehicles and provide extremely dark skies for stargazing.

There are several historic sites throughout the monument. The Josie Morris homestead can be found on the Utah side of the monument and is quite impressive. Josie homesteaded the valley for most of her life and was quite industrious in doing so. The homestead has a cold cellar, chicken coop, house, pond, and orchard on-site.

The monument is home to bighorn sheep, white-tailed prairie dogs (a rare sight), mule deer, the occasional black bear, mountain lions, and more. Several species of endangered fish live within the Green and Yampa Rivers, including the humpback chub, Colorado pikeminnow, razorback sucker, and bonytail chub.

Most of the surrounding land is home to many ranches and farms. You will pass by numerous ranches on your way to the various parts of the monument. Please respect private property as you travel through these areas.

7. DRIVE TO BACKCOUNTRY CAMP IN ECHO PARK

Echo Park is a remote section of Dinosaur National Monument where an especially dark sky makes for magical celestial sights. The campground sits off the bank of the Green River near Steamboat Rock. The Yampa and Green Rivers merge just before the Green wraps around this massive rock.

Activity: Scenic drive to backcountry camping
Adventure rating: 1
Start: Dinosaur National Monument's Dinosaur, Colorado, visitor center
Distance: About 36.92 miles one way
Difficulty: Moderate
Drive time: About 1.5 hours
Best seasons: Late spring, summer, and early fall
Timing: Any time
Fees and permits: $$; campsites are first-come, first-served, $.
Contact: Dinosaur National Monument visitor center, (435) 781-7700
Dog-friendly: No
Road surface: Paved and dirt. You will need a high-clearance 4x4 vehicle.
Land status: National monument
Nearest town: Dinosaur, CO
Other road users: Sheep ranchers, 4-wheelers

Maps: www.nps.gov/dino/planyourvisit/maps.htm
Special considerations: The dirt road becomes impassable when wet. Do not attempt it if there is a prediction of snow or lots of rain. The biting gnats can be unbearable during spring, so come prepared with a head net, the only thing that keeps them out.
Other: This area is very remote. Bring everything you would need to dig yourself out if your vehicle were to get stuck. Make sure you are ready to self-rescue; this might mean backpacking out if necessary.
Supplies to take: Camping gear, vehicle safety supplies, gear necessary to hike out if needed, plenty of food, loads of water, and map and compass or GPS with extra batteries

FINDING THE ROAD

Dinosaur National Monument's Canyon Visitor Center is 2 miles east of Dinosaur, Colorado, just off US 40.
Echo Park Campground GPS: N40 31.254' / W108 59.598'

THE ADVENTURE

From Canyon Visitor Center, take the Harpers Corner Road for just over 25 miles through high meadows and mostly ranchland. Along the way, you'll encounter scenic overlooks to take in a bit more natural and cultural history.

Dropping into Sand Canyon transports you into another world. Soon you will arrive at an abandoned homestead. These old structures were once someone's home and

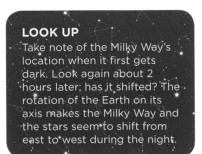

LOOK UP
Take note of the Milky Way's location when it first gets dark. Look again about 2 hours later; has it shifted? The rotation of the Earth on its axis makes the Milky Way and the stars seem to shift from east to west during the night.

Nearby Whispering Cave is quite the experience on a hot summer day. Ducking under a thick wall of sandstone, the cave opens to a narrow passage of about 25 feet. The temperature quickly shifts to about 65°F, quite a change from summertime highs of over 100°F outside the cave.

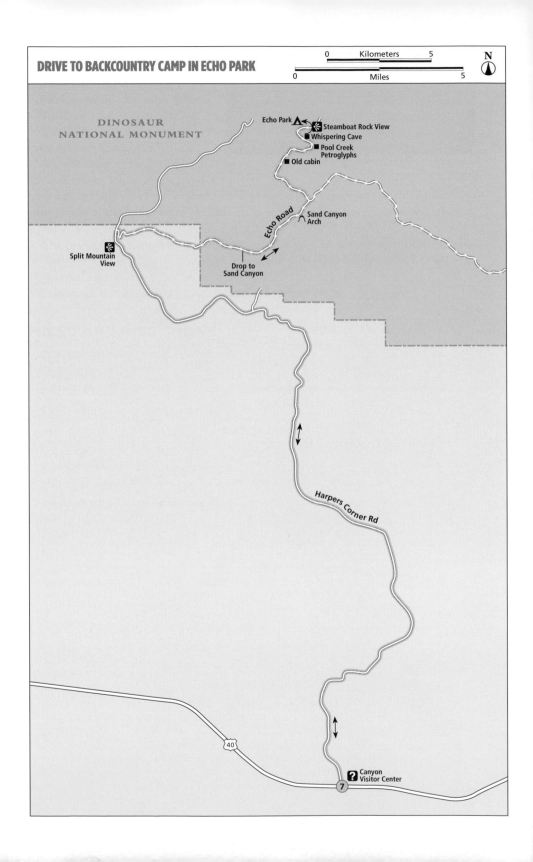

hearth, harking back to a long-gone era. The homestead feels surreal within this rugged landscape.

Pool Creek Petroglyphs are rather unique for this area. The petroglyphs are extremely high up, which shows how much soil has been removed by Pool Creek over the years since the Fremont pecked them. They remind me of pointillism art pieces, with pecked dots making up the characteristic Fremont trapezoidal figures.

After a deep sandy section, a side spur in the road will take you to Whispering Cave. This narrow slit in the cliff wall has a constant temperature in the 60s, providing a welcome respite from the summer heat.

You soon arrive at the campground, on your left. Pick your site and set up camp in your temporary home away from home. At night, take time to visit the river's edge and watch the stars from the soft, sandy shore. Massive Steamboat Rock will be a silhouette with stars all around it on a new moon night. If you hear a loud splash, don't worry; it is most likely a beaver slapping the water with its tail when startled by your presence.

This is one of the most beautiful areas of the monument. Bighorn sheep and mule deer cross through the campground quite frequently due to the remote location and fewer people.

At night the area comes alive as the cosmos emerges above, leaving you spellbound. With little light pollution within the viewshed, the myriad stars make it difficult to pick out constellations. In the summer, the Milky Way stretches above Steamboat Rock, creating a beautiful view of the water, Steamboat Rock, and the arms of the Milky Way Galaxy above.

MILES AND DIRECTIONS

0.0   Start from the Canyon Visitor Center and head north on Harpers Corner Road.

25.03 Split Mountain Overlook, on the right, gives you a beautiful view into the Echo Park region before you begin the drop into the canyon.

25.35 Junction with Echo Park Road. Remember, if there is even a possibility of precipitation, do not drop down into the canyon.

30.06 The road begins to drop into Sand Canyon. The tight curves and scenic views are spectacular.

32.36 Sand Canyon Arch is visible on the north side of the road.

34.83 An abandoned homestead cabin and many outbuildings are visible on each side of the road. This site is worth a quick view before continuing on.

35.84 Arrive at a parking area on the right side of the road. This is the Pool Creek Petroglyphs site, where the ancient petroglyphs are at least 15 to 20 feet above the ground.

36.32 A pull-through parking area on the right offers a quick stop to pop into Whispering Cave. This 25-foot-long fracture in the sandstone has created a nice reprieve from the summer sun.

36.78 Reach the turnoff to Echo Park Campground, a first-come, first-served campground. Before hitting the campground, continue on up the road a short bit to check out Steamboat Rock.

36.92 Arrive at the viewpoint for Steamboat Rock, a massive sandstone monolith that the Green River wraps around on its journey through Dinosaur National Monument.

8. ASTROPHOTOGRAPHY AT SWELTER SHELTER PETROGLYPH

A quick 500 feet from the Tour of Tilted Rocks Scenic Drive (aka Cub Creek Road), you will find the Swelter Shelter, a small alcove that provides little shade from the burning summer sun. This area gets baked by the sun during the day, causing the rock to feel warm deep into the night. The alcove is full of petroglyphs and pictographs created by the Fremont people. The rock is covered in trapezoidal figures and bighorn sheep. The sun, moon, and planets all cross the sky just south of this area.

Activity: Astrophotography
Adventure rating: 1
Start: Swelter Shelter trailhead
Distance: 0.1 mile out and back
Difficulty: Easy
Trip time: 1–6 hours
Best seasons: Any season
Timing: From the quarter moon to the half moon
Fees and permits: $$
Contact: Dinosaur National Monument visitor center, (435) 781-7700
Dog-friendly: No
Trail surface: Dirt

Land status: National monument
Nearest town: Vernal
Other trail users: Hikers
Maps: www.nps.gov/dino/planyourvisit/maps.htm
Special considerations: Petroglyphs and pictographs can be easily damaged by the oils on our hands. Please do not touch these.
Other: Try to avoid the full moon, as it is hard to take longer time lapse shots with so much light.
Supplies to take: Camera, tripod, lenses, and headlamp with extra batteries

FINDING THE TRAILHEAD

From Vernal, follow US 40 headed east for approximately 12.9 miles. Turn left onto UT 149 and drive another 6.9 miles. You will arrive at a small trailhead parking area. The trail is on the north side of the road.
Swelter Shelter Petroglyph Trailhead
GPS: N 40.43693° / W 109.29216°

The pigments needed for pictographs were created by the Fremont using the resources at hand. Plant pigments were often used to create the beautiful paints.

Other Opportunities to Enjoy the Night Sky
PARK RANGER–LED EVENTS
During spring, summer, and fall, the park offers star parties. These evening events highlight the night sky found within the park and offer the opportunity to look through a telescope at deep space objects such as nebulae, galaxies, star clusters, and more. For more information on the timing of these events, visit www.nps.gov/dino/planyourvisit/calendar.htm.

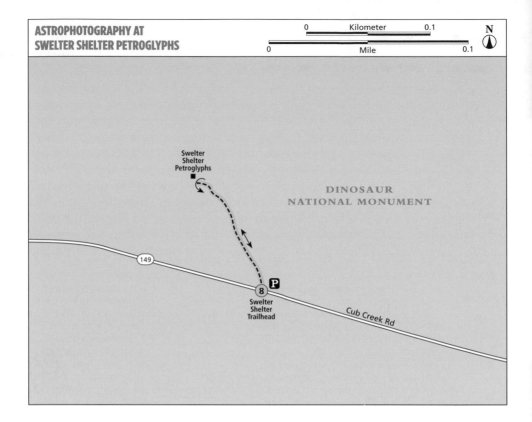

THE ADVENTURE

Head up the short trail to the raised area beneath the petroglyphs. Once there, find your favorite position for photographing a few of the pictographs or petroglyphs while capturing a sliver of night sky as well. Set up your equipment and enjoy the process.

STEINAKER STATE PARK

Location: 4335 N. Hwy. 191, Vernal, UT 84078
Cost: $
Dark Sky designation: 2018

Contact: (435) 789-4432
Land status: State park
Maps: https://stateparks.utah.gov/parks/steinaker/directions/

STEINAKER RESERVOIR IS A FISHING HAVEN stocked with bluegill, green sunfish, largemouth bass, and rainbow trout. It is also a popular park for waterskiing, paddling, and swimming. During the warmer months, the park has incredible stargazing. Camping during the spring, summer, and fall is also quite popular.

Along the shores of Steinaker Reservoir, fossils of ancient sea life such as oysters, clams, and shellfish can be found. Nearby Dinosaur National Monument, where fossils of more than 500 individual dinosaurs were discovered, is a huge draw for area visitors.

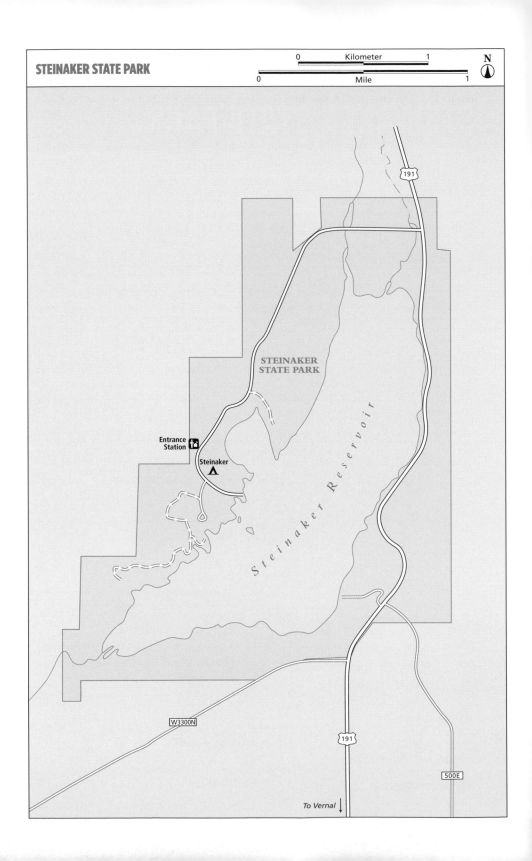

The bench that the town of Vernal sits on had long been the hunting grounds of the Uintah people. In 1861, Abraham Lincoln set the area aside as the Uintah Indian Reservation. The area was first settled by European-Americans who made their living as trappers and prospectors. A few homesteaders eventually settled the area as well. Many of these early settlers were ranchers and farmers producing cattle, sheep, honey, grains, and alfalfa.

In 1915, Dinosaur National Monument was created to protect the dinosaur skeletons found within the 80 acres around the current Quarry site. Over the years, the monument grew to nearly 211,000 acres. In 1948, oil was discovered in the Vernal area, which began a growth boom for the community. The boom-and-bust nature of the oil industry has historically caused problems for rural communities. Vernal's agricultural resources and Dinosaur National Monument's tourism draw have sustained the community during the times when the oil industry was in a bust.

9. OVERNIGHT STAY IN DIPPY CABIN

From mid-March to mid-October, Dippy Cabin, or Dilopharsus Cabin, is open for business. The small cabin sits within Steinaker Campground and houses six people comfortably, with eight being the limit. The cabin overlooks the reservoir for quite a scenic view. It has a queen-size bunk bed with an additional futon bed for sleeping and a table for four. Additional amenities are a mini fridge and small microwave. Outside is a picnic table, charcoal stand, and fire pit. Water is available in the campground.

At night the stars steal the show. The night sky is filled with many pinpricks of light, making it difficult to make out constellations.

Activity: Cabin stay
Adventure rating: 1
Start: Steinaker State Park
Distance: None
Difficulty: Easy
Best seasons: Spring, summer, and fall
Timing: Any time of the month
Fees and permits: $$$
Contact: Steinaker State Park, (435) 789-4432
Dog-friendly: No
Land status: State park
Nearest town: Vernal

Maps: https://stateparks.utah.gov/parks/steinaker/directions/
Special considerations: Reservations are best for this one; you can make them 4 months in advance.
Other: There is a charge for extra vehicles, so try to carpool.
Supplies to take: General camping equipment including dishes and bedding for the cabin beds; outdoor chairs for stargazing; binoculars for night sky viewing; night sky map or app; daytime equipment to play on the reservoir

FINDING THE CABIN

From Vernal, follow US 191 north for 5.6 miles. Turn left onto UT 301 for another 1.8 miles. Turn left and Steinaker Campground is about 0.3 mile.
Steinaker State Park GPS: N40 31.119' / W109 32.544'

THE ADVENTURE

This is a simple adventure. After dark, go outside and find a clear spot to set up your camp chair. Use your night sky map and binoculars to view the brighter objects on the map. If you'd rather, just relax and enjoy the show!

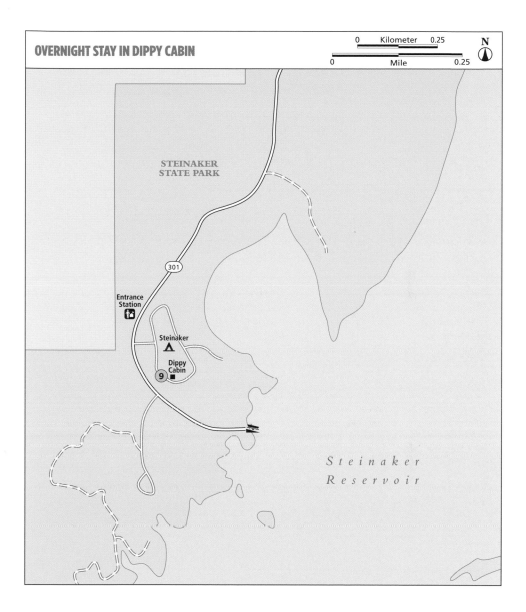

Other Opportunities to Enjoy the Night Sky
PARK RANGER–LED EVENTS
During spring, summer, and fall, the park offers star parties. These evening events highlight the night sky found within the park and offer the opportunity to look through a telescope at deep space objects such as nebulae, galaxies, star clusters, and more. For more information on the timing of these events, visit https://stateparks.utah.gov/parks/steinaker/events/.

SOUTHWEST UTAH

SOUTHWESTERN UTAH IS HOME TO THE MOJAVE DESERT, a vast hot desert with life-forms—from scorpions to Gila monsters—as unique and incredible as the geography of the area. Desert tortoises call the Mojave home as well, wandering the desert looking for flower blooms and forbs to eat. The area also hosts mule deer, bighorn sheep, coyotes, bobcats, roadrunners, owls, many species of lizards, hares, rabbits, and many rodents.

From the iconic Joshua trees to the sweet-smelling creosote bushes, the landscape begins to look like a cartoon desert. Agave plants rise from the soil with their swordlike leaves protected by sharp needles. Beavertail cactus covers full sun–exposed areas, while hedgehog cactus fills in the rocky slopes.

Volcanic cinder cones cover much of this region of Utah. The flow of lava, some of it forming caves, can still be seen across most of the region in the massive basalt fields. The massive Pine Mountains, north of St. George, are laccolithic mountains, formed when the flow of lava spreads out along a weak underground layer and creates a mushroom of lava below the surface of the Earth's crust. This spread reduces pressure, preventing an eruption from happening.

The land was once wandered by the Ancestral Puebloan people, and the petroglyphs they created can still be found. The Nuwuvi (Southern Paiute) and descendants of the Puebloan people have long called the Mojave Desert home, and today use resources from the harsh landscape as their ancestors did before them.

In the 1860s, settlers came to the area to establish farms and ranches throughout southwest Utah. The harsh realities of the desert soon became evident: Flash flooding after the intense rains of monsoon season is known to have taken out some homesteads, and drought conditions destroyed crops during the relentless summers. Their tenacious spirit is seen today in the various small communities scattered throughout this part of Utah.

Today the national and state parks within this area provide spaces for area residents and visitors to relax and rejuvenate their souls surrounded by spectacular settings. Whether on horseback through the Pine Mountains or Dixie National Forest, backpacking or hiking along the trails within the parks, canyoneering through slot canyons, climbing the sandstone cliffs, or just relaxing in the shade, you are surrounded by grandeur.

ZION NATIONAL PARK

Location: 1 Zion Park Blvd., State Route 9, Springdale, UT 84767
Cost: $$$
Dark Sky designation: In progress

Contact: Zion National Park visitor center, (435) 772-3256
Land status: National park
Maps: www.nps.gov/zion/planyourvisit/maps.htm

WHETHER YOU ARE DRAWN TO ZION NATIONAL PARK for the massive sandstone monoliths towering above Zion Canyon and the Virgin River or prefer to explore one of the park's many slot canyons, you are sure to be left speechless. Words cannot describe the beauty contained within this landscape. The brilliant turquoise-blue water of the Virgin River is striking in contrast with the orange walls within the canyon.

Above the rim of Zion Canyon, in the meadows that surround it, you might encounter an elk, black bear, coyote, peregrine falcon, or mountain lion. Giant ponderosa pines, mountain maples, aspens, and mountain shrubs and grasses grow as moisture and need dictate.

Within the canyon walls, mountain lions, mule deer, bats, insects, ringtails, tarantulas, rabbits, and many rodents call the valley home. Seeps within these walls host columbine, maidenhair ferns, and a variety of mosses. Yucca, brittlebush, shadscale, and other shrubs fill in the rocky hillsides.

Along the river corridor, toads, tree frogs, mountain lions, skunks, ringtails, squirrels, and many species of native fish inhabit the area. The river corridor is lined with massive

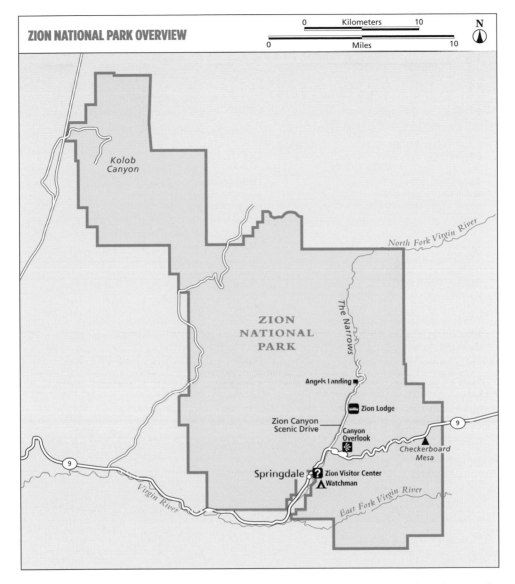

Kilometers

Miles

N

Kolob
Canyon

North Fork Virgin River

The Narrows

ZION
NATIONAL
PARK

Angels Landing

Zion Lodge

Zion Canyon
Scenic Drive

Canyon
Overlook

9

Checkerboard
Mesa

Springdale

Zion Visitor Center

Watchman

9

Virgin River

East Fork Virgin River

cottonwoods that provide crucial shade during the hot summer months and water for area wildlife. Along the river, you will also find the two campgrounds within the park.

The Virgin River has carved deep into the porous sandstone for millions of years, creating the popular Narrows region of the park. The Narrows is a section of the river that is bordered by sheer cliffs on both sides, with much of the river being knee deep.

Just about everywhere you look, you can see where water runs off the cliffs, over the hillsides, along washes, and toward the river below. During monsoon season, flash floods seem to come off the cliffs in every direction, most carrying more debris than water. Being mindful of the weather is crucial when down in the valley and its slot canyons.

With three levels of elevation to explore, no matter what you choose to do, the park is sure to dazzle. Recreate responsibly and enjoy.

10. NIGHT BICYCLE RIDE ON PA'RUS TRAIL

Cycling along the Pa'rus Trail under the stars, feeling the wind caress your skin, is exhilarating. The sound of the river seems to reverberate off the nearby hillside. The three bridge crossings provide a quick glimpse of water, stars, and trees.

Activity: Night bicycle ride
Adventure rating: 1
Start: Zion National Park visitor center or historical marker parking on UT 9
Distance: 3.5 miles out and back
Elevation gain: 415 feet
Difficulty: Easy
Riding time: About 30 minutes
Best seasons: Spring, summer, and fall
Timing: Any time of the month
Fees and permits: $$$
Contact: Zion National Park visitor center, (435) 772-3256
Dog-friendly: No
Trail surface: Concrete with metal bridges
Land status: National park
Nearest town: Springdale

Other trail users: Hikers, walkers, skateboarders, roller skaters
Maps: www.nps.gov/zion/planyourvisit/maps.htm
Special considerations: In the early morning and late evening during the spring and fall, the trail and bridges may become ice covered. Use caution, and check trail conditions before heading out.
Other: Watch out for holes in the concrete. Stay together in a group when traveling at night. You can also start this ride at the other end, at the historical marker along UT 9 near the bridge.
Supplies to take: Water, bicycle, headlamp with extra batteries, bike headlight and taillight, helmet, hand pump, and patch kit

FINDING THE TRAILHEAD

From Springdale, follow UT 9 north for 1.2 miles. Turn right into the visitor center area about 0.2 mile. Park within the parking lot and walk back to the west side of the visitor center to find the trailhead.
Zion National Park visitor center GPS: N37 11.999' / W112 59.223'

THE ADVENTURE

Head to the west side of the visitor center and follow the sidewalk north to where it crosses the road leading into the area. Across the road is the start of the Pa'rus Trail. The first section of trail moves between the campground and river.

Just north of the campground, a trail to the left leads to the Zion Nature Center parking lot. From here on, you will be alone until reaching the bridge area along UT 9.

Continue riding north. You cross two more bridges like the first one, then there is a brief straightaway before you ride under the UT 9 bridge and come to Zion Canyon Scenic Drive. This is your turnaround point. Enjoy the warm night air, stars, and silhouetted monoliths as you head back to the visitor center parking lot.

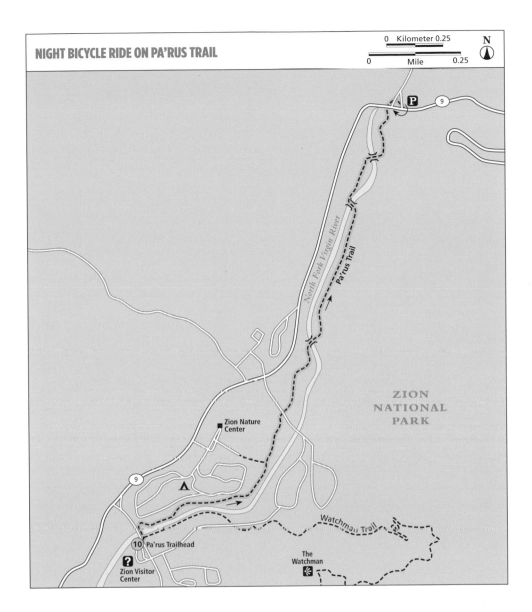

NIGHT BICYCLE RIDE ON PA'RUS TRAIL

MILES AND DIRECTIONS

0.0 Start at the Pa'rus trailhead.

0.46 Junction with trail to nature center.

0.83 First bridge crossing; this is a great place to take in the view.

1.3 Second bridge crossing.

1.45 Third bridge crossing.

1.66 Pa'rus Trail ends.

1.75 Historical marker parking; turn around here.

3.5 Arrive back at the Pa'rus trailhead.

Pa'rus is a Nuwuvi (Southern Paiute) word meaning "bubbling, tumbling water." The name was adopted to describe the Virgin River as it moves through the rocky streambed.

LOOK UP

When you reach the first bridge crossing, take a moment to look up and back the way you came. You can see the Watchman on river left, the Virgin River underneath the bridge, and the arm of Milky Way above. This stunning vista is one of the most photographed views with astrophotographers visiting Zion.

11. FULL MOON HIKE TO CANYON OVERLOOK

Easily one of the best views of Zion Canyon can be found at the Canyon Overlook. This short trail takes you to the 2,200-foot cliff edge, which looks out over the Mount Carmel Highway and the many switchbacks that guide vehicles down to the Virgin River valley. Beyond, you can see the Court of the Patriarchs.

Activity: Full moon hike
Adventure rating: 2
Start: Canyon Overlook trailhead
Distance: 0.78 mile out and back
Elevation gain: 144 feet
Difficulty: Easy
Hiking time: About 45 minutes
Best seasons: Spring, summer, and fall
Timing: Any time of the month
Fees and permits: $$$
Trail contact: Zion National Park visitor center, (435) 772-3256
Dog-friendly: No
Trail surface: Stone and dirt
Land status: National park

Nearest town: Springdale
Other trail users: None
Maps: www.nps.gov/zion/planyourvisit/maps.htm
Special considerations: In the early morning and late evening during the spring and fall, the trail may become ice covered. Use caution, and check trail conditions before heading out.
Other: This trail has a lot of exposure. Keep your limits in mind, and use caution.
Supplies to take: Water, headlamp with extra batteries, layers of clothing, night sky map, and hiking boots with good traction

FINDING THE TRAILHEAD

From Springdale, head north on UT 9 for 7 miles to the Canyon Overlook trailhead. The road will pass the entrance gates, then climb up a series of switchback, and finally move through a few tunnels before coming to the trailhead, on the right after the last tunnel.

Canyon Overlook trailhead GPS: N37 12.802' / W112 56.448'

THE ADVENTURE

The trail begins with a quick climb across the sandstone to a set of rock stairs, which will account for the majority of elevation gain on this hike. Once past the stairs, the trail becomes a bit exposed, with a few exterior sections of trail connected to the cliff wall.

After passing a natural seep in the rock, you will come to a section with exposure to your left. Keep in mind that there is no barrier in this location; proceed with caution. Once through this section, the trail moves onto sandstone. Follow the sandstone around and down to the overlook.

A gentle descent along the sandstone leads to the end of the trail and Canyon Overlook. You are now standing 2,200 feet above the valley floor. Just left of center, you can see headlights from cars forming a ribbon of light as they descend to Zion Canyon.

> **LOOK UP**
> The dark areas on the moon are actually basalt fields, not the smooth surface it appears to be from Earth.

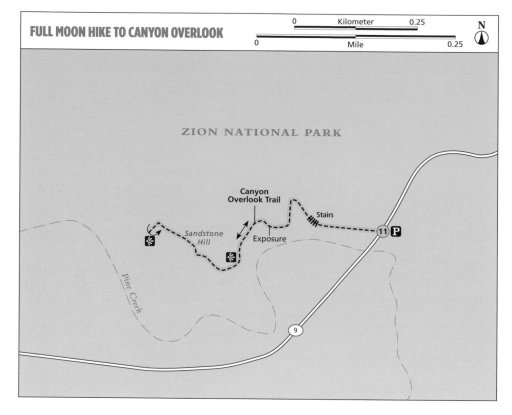

ZION NATIONAL PARK

Canyon
Overlook Trail

Stairs

Sandstone
Hill

Exposure

Pine Creek

11 P

9

The sandstone has a lovely slope, providing the perfect opportunity to lie back and take in the moonlight and a few of the brighter stars. After you have had enough stargazing, head back the way you came.

MILES AND DIRECTIONS

0.0 Start at the Canyon Overlook trailhead.

0.07 Climb a set of rock stairs.

0.17 Exposed section begins; use caution.

0.32 Descend on sandstone to overlook.

0.39 Welcome to the Canyon Overlook! After enjoying the view and the skies, retrace your steps the way you came.

0.78 Arrive back the Canyon Overlook trailhead.

> The trail moves through a nice desert seep, a natural spring emerging from the rock. You can usually hear drops of water fall when it is quiet.

12. ASTROPHOTOGRAPHY FROM BRIDGE ON PA'RUS TRAIL

One of the icons of Zion National Park, the Watchman is a jagged-looking peak watching over the valley below, named for its position as guardian over the Springdale community. Its orange color provides the perfect backdrop to the turquoise of the Virgin River during the day. At night the silhouette of the Watchman juts out from the cliffside, while the river seems to shine as it moves around stones. The best spot to get this photo where the Watchman is quite large in the background is from the first bridge north of the nature center.

Activity: Astrophotography
Adventure rating: 1
Start: Zion Nature Center picnic area
Distance: 1.04 miles out and back
Elevation gain: 26 feet
Difficulty: Easy
Trip time: About 30 minutes
Best seasons: Any season
Timing: Any time of the month or night
Fees and permits: $$$
Trail contact: Zion National Park visitor center, (435) 772-3256
Dog-friendly: No
Trail surface: Concrete with metal bridges
Land status: National park

Nearest town: Springdale
Other trail users: Bicyclists, hikers
Maps: www.nps.gov/zion/planyourvisit/maps.htm
Special considerations: In the early morning and late evening during the spring and fall, the trail and bridge may become ice covered. Use caution, and check trail conditions the day before you plan to hike.
Other: Bring a headlamp with red light capability.
Supplies to take: Water, headlamp with extra batteries, camera equipment and tripod, and layers of clothing

FINDING THE TRAILHEAD

From Springdale, head north on UT 9 for 1.5 miles to the entrance station. Once through the entrance station, continue up UT 9 for another 0.3 mile, then turn right into the nature center area. After driving a few hundred feet, turn left and drive about 500 feet to a slight right for 0.2 mile to the picnic parking area. The trailhead is on the northeast side of the parking area.
Zion Nature Center picnic area GPS: N37 12.284' / W112 58.988'

THE ADVENTURE

If you chose to photograph during the early morning hours, you will most likely be alone and the bridge will not vibrate as when others cross on bicycles. There are some perks to being an early riser. Wildlife sightings are more frequent in the early morning hours too.

Once you've loaded up your backpack with all the necessary camera and safety gear, head toward the amphitheater, then continue straight until you run into the Pa'rus Trail. Head north along the Pa'rus Trail to the first bridge.

This bridge will be your setting for photography. Set up your camera equipment and begin the shoot. During the summer months, with a bit of patience, the Milky Way will line up with the river, creating an incredible view of the canyon, the river, and the arm of the Milky Way Galaxy. Once you've captured that perfect shot, head back the way you came.

LOOK UP
An hour before the sun crests over the horizon is referred to as the "blue hour" by astrophotographers. The sky starts to shift from black to blue, and the first rays of sunlight begin to light up the atmosphere, showing stars and blue sky in photographs.

Other Opportunities to Enjoy the Night Sky
PARK RANGER–LED EVENTS
During spring, summer, and fall, the park offers star parties. These evening events highlight the night sky found within the park and offer the opportunity to look through a telescope at deep space objects such as nebulae, galaxies, star clusters, and more. For more information on the timing of these events, visit www.nps.gov/zion/planyourvisit/calendar.htm.

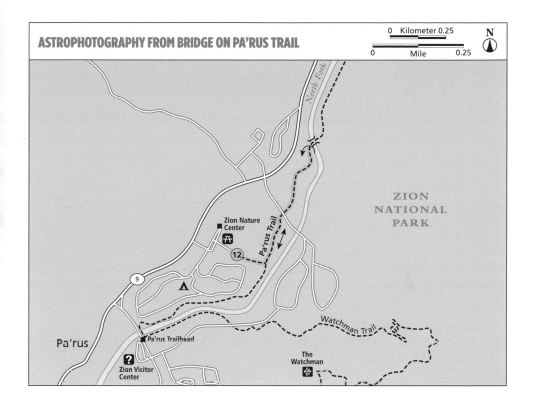

MILES AND DIRECTIONS

0.0 Start at the nature center picnic area.

0.16 Junction with Pa'rus Trail. Turn left.

0.52 Bridge and scene for astrophotography. Return the way you came.

1.04 Arrive back at the picnic area.

SPRINGDALE

Location: Springdale Town Offices, 118 Lion Blvd., Springdale, UT 84767
Dark Sky designation: Not designated

Contact: Springdale town offices, (435) 772-3434
Land status: Municipal
Maps: www.zionpark.com

RESTING ON THE SOUTHERN BORDER OF ZION NATIONAL PARK, the town of Springdale is home to an estimated 500 year-round residents. Largely supported by its tourism economy, with several million visitors drawn to Zion National Park each year, this quaint desert community is teeming with life during the spring, summer, fall, and most holidays in the winter months.

The first people to call Zion Canyon home were the Archaic people in about AD 500. The indigenous community thrived here through the Ancestral Puebloan people. In about AD 1200, a major drought forced the Puebloan people to move south to a more temperate climate. Eventually the Nuwuvi (Southern Paiute) people returned to their ancestral lands, and they continue to live on nearby reservation lands today. When

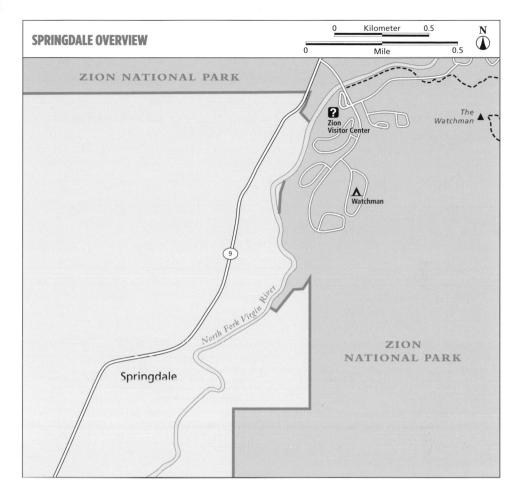

ZION NATIONAL PARK

Zion Visitor Center

The Watchman

Watchman

9

North Fork Virgin River

ZION NATIONAL PARK

Springdale

0   Kilometer   0.5

0   Mile   0.5

N

Dominguez and Escalante traveled through the canyon, they found the Nuwuvi (Southern Paiute) people cultivating crops throughout the Virgin River valley.

In the mid-1860s, homesteaders moved into the valley and created the small community of Springdale. These early homesteaders quickly learned the reality of living in the harsh desert environment. Flash flooding after monsoon rains is common to this region, and landslides happen from time to time.

> Mukuntuweap is the Nuwuvi (Southern Paiute) word for "straight canyon." The name was later changed to Zion National Park.

In 1917, groups of tourists begin to arrive in the valley with the improvement of roads and vehicles. By 1920 the community would be forever changed by the creation of Mukuntuweap National Monument.

Today Springdale is the adventure hub community for tourists visiting the park. Plan well in advance of your vacation to ensure that you can access all the areas of the park you'd like for a wonderful trip.

13. SUNRISE FROM THE WATCHMAN

Get an early start for this one in order to take in a few stars before they become washed out as sunlight returns to this side of the Earth. Taking in a Zion Canyon sunrise from an elevated location is awe-inspiring! The pink of the clouds seems to reflect from within the rocks themselves. The Court of the Patriarchs is in session, waiting for the return of light to its bleached white surface.

Activity: Early morning hike
Adventure rating: 2
Start: Zion National Park visitor center
Distance: 3.11 miles out and back
Elevation gain: 739 feet
Difficulty: Moderate
Hiking time: About 3 hours
Best seasons: Spring, summer, and fall
Timing: Any time of the month
Fees and permits: $$$
Trail contact: Zion National Park visitor center, (435) 772-3256
Dog-friendly: No
Trail surface: Dirt
Land status: National park

Nearest town: Springdale
Other trail users: None
Maps: www.nps.gov/zion/planyourvisit/maps.htm
Special considerations: In the early morning and late evening during the spring and fall, the trail may become ice covered. Use caution, and check trail conditions the day before you plan to hike.
Other: Hiking boots are highly suggested due to uneven terrain.
Supplies to take: Water, salty snacks, headlamp with extra batteries, and layers of clothing. Once that sun pops up, the temperature can change quickly.

FINDING THE TRAILHEAD
From Springdale, follow UT 9 north for 1.2 miles. Turn right into the visitor center area about 0.2 mile. Park within the parking lot and walk back to the west side of the visitor center to find the trailhead.
Zion National Park visitor center GPS: N37 11.999' / W112 59.223'

THE ADVENTURE
The summit loop provides incredible views of the Virgin River valley and Springdale bisected by the Virgin River as it flows south. If you look north up Zion Canyon, you can see the of Angels Landing formation jutting out into the valley. This beautiful formation makes for a sketchy hike following chains to the small summit, but it's definitely worth it, as the views are stellar.

> Sol is the name of our solar system's star—a middle-aged yellow star that is predicted to burn happily for another 5 billion years.

You'll have to start early to catch the sunrise at the summit. It takes on average about 1.5 hours to climb up to the overlook. Plan your hike accordingly.

Walk to the west side of the visitor center and follow the sidewalk north to where you will see the trailhead for both the Pa'rus Trail and the Watchman Trail. Make sure you

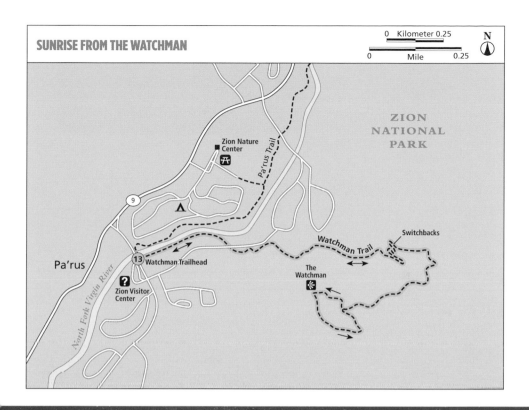

SUNRISE FROM THE WATCHMAN

ZION NATIONAL PARK

Zion Nature Center

Pa'rus Trail

9

Pa'rus

North Fork Virgin River

13 Watchman Trailhead

Zion Visitor Center

Watchman Trail

Switchbacks

The Watchman

take the correct trail; it should follow the east side of the river for
the first bit.

As you begin the hike, there
will still be a few stars out. It will
begin to become light about 1
hour before sunrise.

After leading through the flat,
the trail begins to climb as it goes

LOOK UP
Which star will be the last you can see before sunlight returns to the valley? Take a moment to see what constellations you recognize when, in the flat along the east side of the Virgin River.

back into a ravine. Along the climb, you'll have a few opportunities to take in the view and the last of the stars. Follow the trail up to the top, where a small loop will take you to the best views.

The north side of the loop provides views of Zion Canyon; the west side has views of the Virgin River valley and Springdale; and the south side has a beautiful view of the Watchman, the famous sentry of Zion Canyon.

Head back the way you came to complete the hike.

MILES AND DIRECTIONS

0.0   Start from the Watchman trailhead.

0.28 Cross a road.

0.77 Switchbacks aid in climbing quickly in elevation.

1.36 Reach the loop junction and bear right.

1.48 Views of the Watchman, Zion Canyon, and Springdale.

1.74 Reach the loop junction once more and your return trail to the visitor center.

2.34 Descend through the switchbacks.

2.84 Cross the road.

3.11   Arrive back at the Watchman trailhead.

BRYCE CANYON NATIONAL PARK

Location: PO Box 640201, Bryce, UT 84764
Cost: $$$
Dark Sky designation: 2019

Contact: Bryce Canyon National Park visitor center, (435) 834-5322
Land status: National park
Maps: www.nps.gov/brca/planyourvisit/maps.htm

WHENEVER I VISIT BRYCE CANYON NATIONAL PARK, the landscape reminds me of being in a woodcarver's shop. Well, a woodcarver who has a hard time finishing a piece so moves on to the next piece instead. Everywhere you look in Bryce, there are hoodoos stacked side by side, unfinished pieces of work being carved by the natural forces of water, weathering, and wind.

Bryce Canyon National Park is most easily accessed by a road along the mesa top. From that vantage point, visitors are able to look down into the canyons below. Canyons

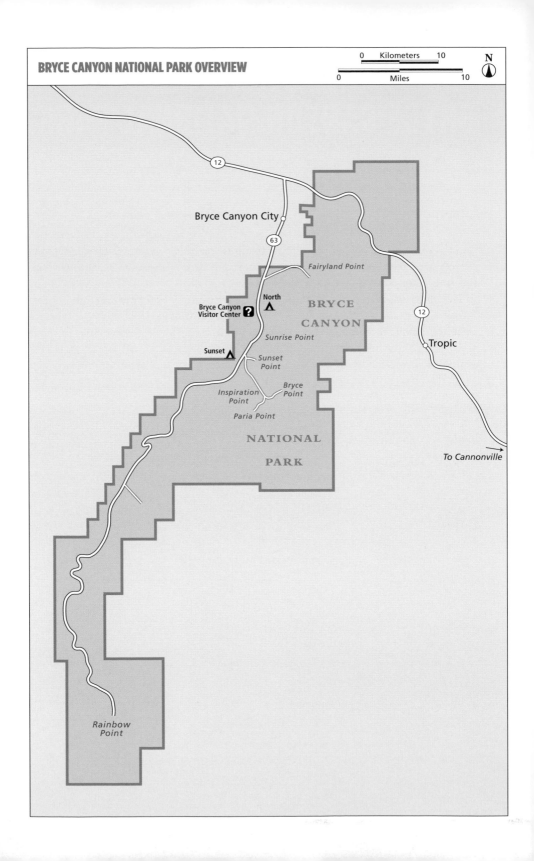

0   Kilometers   10

0   Miles   10

N

12

Bryce Canyon City

63

Fairyland Point

North

Bryce Canyon
Visitor Center ?

**BRYCE
CANYON**

Sunrise Point

12

Sunset

*Sunset
Point*

Tropic

*Inspiration
Point*

*Bryce
Point*

Paria Point

NATIONAL

PARK

To Cannonville

*Rainbow
Point*

Feeding wild animals can lead to aggressive, unruly behavior from these otherwise self-sufficient critters. It may also lead to unnatural competition for food and battles between species that normally get along fine.

of orange soil and cream-colored hoodoos in every bowl below the mesa's rim complement the deep green of the park's ponderosa forests.

The park is home to black bears, deer, mountain lions, pronghorn, coyotes, foxes, peregrine falcons, and a wide variety of birds and small mammals. Steller's jays, ravens, squirrels, and chipmunks are all likely to beg for food if you spend time in the campground or at the picnic areas and overlooks.

The Utah prairie dog, once an endangered species in the United States, may on occasion be seen flinging soil out of a burrow that it is currently excavating. They build new burrows frequently, an activity that allows water to seep into the ground easily and softens the ground for other plants and animals.

The Bryce Canyon area has been visited for at least 10,000 years. Archaic people followed the migration of area megafauna to hunt following the last ice age. Ancestral Puebloan people moved through this area hunting and foraging until the drought between AD 1200 and 1300. The Nuwuvi (Southern Paiute) people ventured to the higher elevations to collect pine nuts and hunt rabbits.

Pine nuts are an energy-packed nut found in the pinecones of pinyon trees.

In the late 1800s, homesteaders moved to this area to live, creating irrigation systems, leading from the higher elevations of present-day Dixie National Forest to the lower elevations near Tropic, to provide the water needed for agriculture and ranching.

Bryce Canyon National Park was designated in 1924 but wouldn't see many visitors until after the Union Pacific Railroad and the Civilian Conservation Corps made the area more accessible to vehicles. Much of the CCC's stonework can still be seen. Today the park hosts about 1.5 million visitors per year, most of that during the summer months.

14. **NIGHT HIKE ON NAVAJO LOOP**

This steep hike highlights what Bryce Canyon National Park is famous for: hoodoos. One of the main features is a hoodoo top that looks like and is named Thor's Hammer. Then come the twins—twin windows and twin natural bridges are the next few formations to delight the eyes. A walk through a ponderosa and fir forest is followed by feeling dwarfed by the hoodoo skyscrapers stretching up into the night sky. The view of stars filling in the narrow slit of sky while walking through the steep-walled, narrow passages is quite something to behold. Ponderosa pines stretch to touch the night sky. Along this hike, it quickly becomes a game of what natural frame is best for viewing the night sky. I'm certain you will find that all of them succeed in different ways.

Activity: Night hike
Adventure rating: 1
Start: Sunset Point
Distance: 1.19-mile loop
Elevation gain: 498 feet
Difficulty: Moderate
Trip time: About 1 hour
Best seasons: Summer
Timing: On the new moon or a few days after the full moon
Fees and permits: $$$
Contact: Bryce Canyon National Park visitor center, (435) 834-5322
Dog-friendly: No
Trail surface: Dirt
Land status: National park
Nearest town: Bryce City

Other trail users: None
Maps: www.nps.gov/brca/planyourvisit/maps.htm
Special considerations: The entire loop is only open during the summer months. Plan accordingly if you'd like to complete the whole adventure. Due to ice building up on the trail, during the snowy months the trail will be an out-and-back only.
Other: Hiking boots are highly suggested due to uneven terrain.
Supplies to take: Water, salty snacks, headlamp with extra batteries, and layers of clothing. The temperature can change quickly at higher elevations.

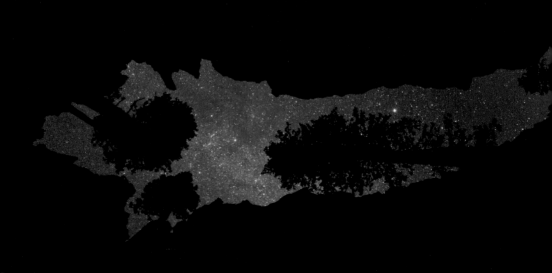

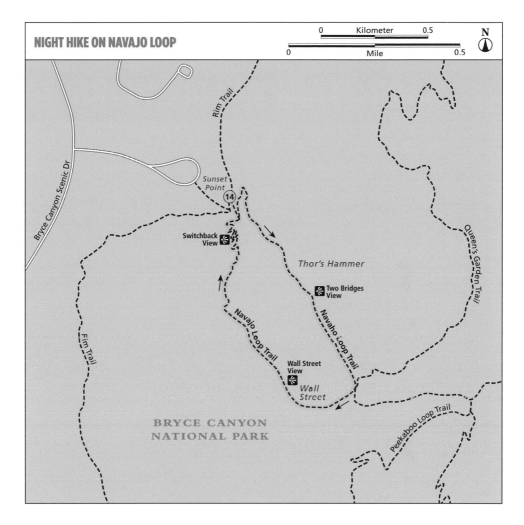

FINDING THE TRAILHEAD

From Tropic head west on UT 12 for 7.4 miles. Turn left onto UT 63 and drive another 2.6 miles to Bryce Canyon National Park. Once you have passed the entrance gate, drive another 2.3 miles to the turn for Sunset Point. Turn left and drive 0.2 mile to the trailhead.

Sunset Point GPS: N37 37.366' / W112 09.978'

THE ADVENTURE

Once you've parked, grab your pack and head out to Sunset Point. At Sunset Point, take the northern route of the Navajo Loop Trail. It will drop quickly down a set of switchbacks. You should see the silhouette of Thor's Hammer and the twin windows on the climb down. As the trail narrows, you hike through ponderosa pines stretching up into the sky with cliff walls on both sides. A little farther

> Thor's Hammer is a capstone, a harder stone that erodes slower than the stone it rests on.

on, you will come across the twin bridges before hitting the lower valley.

Once in the valley, stay on the Navajo Loop Trail as you wander through a conifer forest and continue the climb back up through Wall Street, a narrow area with massive hoodoos looking much like massive skyscrapers. Continue up the trail as you return to the mesa above. The trail has a few switchbacks on the final section of the climb.

LOOK UP

New York City is a Bortle scale Class 9 night sky, the most light pollution possible. You are now in a Bortle Class 2 site. Look at all those stars.

MILES AND DIRECTIONS

0.0 Start at Sunset Point; the first few hundred feet are filled by a long switchback in the trail.

0.35 Two natural bridges span the trail.

0.7 At Wall Street, look up and take in the staggering height of the hoodoos above.

1.13 Climb a few switchbacks before the rim.

1.19 Arrive back at Sunset Point.

15. NIGHT NORDIC SKI TO PARIA AND BRYCE POINTS

With the majority of life sleeping away the cold winter night, the silence is astonishing. As you ski along, the only sounds you will most likely hear are your skis moving through the snow. Above, a sky full of stars is revealed, outlined by tall conifers. The occasional hoot of an owl may be heard during the early night. Seeing the silhouettes of hoodoos and trees by starlight or moonlight is beautiful. The climb to Bryce Point is just enough to get warmed up and ready to go. It's a quick drop in elevation with a short climb at the end to Paria Point. With the majority of this route being downhill, a nice kick and glide will do for much of the route.

Activity: Night Nordic ski
Adventure rating: 2
Start: Winter ski parking area for Bryce Point
Distance: 4.63 miles out and back
Elevation gain: 425 feet
Difficulty: Moderate
Trip time: About 1.5 hours
Best seasons: Winter
Timing: Any time of the night
Fees and permits: $$$
Contact: Bryce Canyon National Park visitor center, (435) 834-5322
Dog-friendly: No

Trail surface: Snow
Land status: National park
Nearest town: Bryce City
Other trail users: Snowshoers
Maps: www.nps.gov/brca/ planyourvisit/maps.htm
Special considerations: This ski route is only open during the winter months when snow is deep enough.
Supplies to take: Water, salty snacks, headlamp with extra batteries, Nordic ski gear, and layers of clothing. The temperature can change quickly at higher elevations.

FINDING THE TRAILHEAD

From Tropic head west on UT 12 for 7.4 miles. Turn left onto UT 63 and drive another 2.6 miles to Bryce Canyon National Park. Once you have passed the entrance gate, drive another 2.8 miles to the turn for Sunset Point. Turn left and park in the winter trailhead.

Bryce Point Road GPS: N37 36.997' / W112 10.489'

THE ADVENTURE

Gear up and strap on the skis. Don't forget your head-lamp with extra batteries. It's time to glide through a snowy wonderland filled with stars. The first mile is a lovely kick and glide to get your muscles warmed up.

After you pass the junction for Paria Point, the trail will climb to Bryce Point. The grade is fine though and will require just a bit more kick to power up. At about the 2-mile mark, you will reach Bryce Point. Seeing the hoodoos by moonlight is an extraordinary experience.

> A nice trick to prewarm your legs is to add a few drops of clove oil to lotion and rub it on your legs before heading out.

LOOK UP

Can you find the constellation Gemini
in the night sky? The second-brightest
star in Gemini is Castor. Stars more
commonly come in binary pairs. Castor
is a six-star system—three sets of
binary stars in a beautiful dance around
a common center point of gravity.

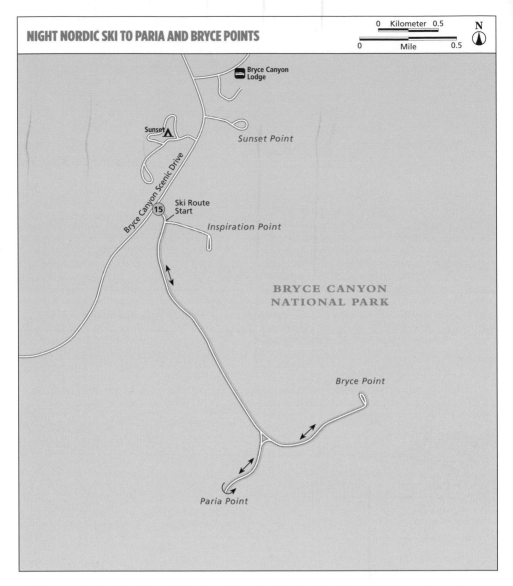

0   Kilometer 0.5

0   Mile   0.5

N

Bryce Canyon
Lodge

Sunset

Sunset Point

Bryce Canyon Scenic Drive

15 Ski Route
Start

Inspiration Point

BRYCE CANYON
NATIONAL PARK

Bryce Point

Paria Point

When ready, head back and take the quick mile climb to Paria Point. Back on the main trail, enjoy the slight descent to your vehicle.

MILES AND DIRECTIONS

0.0 Start at the Bryce Point Road winter parking area.

1.29 Junction with Paria Point Road; head for Bryce Point.

1.95 The climb ends at Bryce Point, the highest elevation in the adventure.

2.94 Reach Paria Point after a quick downhill.

3.34 Junction with Bryce Point Road; turn left and enjoy the glide back.

4.63 Arrive back at the parking area.

16. ASTROPHOTOGRAPHY ON SUNSET POINT

While standing on the rim's edge on Sunset Point, to the north and south you can see bowls full of hoodoos below the mesa rim. On a moonlit night, these natural bowls will show up in photographs as if it is daylight, with the cream and orange colors showing brightly. The sky will hold quite a few stars in a light blue sky. To capture more stars and less color, pick a night near the first quarter moon.

Activity: Astrophotography
Adventure rating: 1
Start: Sunset Point
Distance: None
Difficulty: Easy
Trip time: 1-6 hours
Best seasons: Any season
Timing: A few days after the full moon to the new moon
Fees and permits: $$$
Trail contact: Bryce Canyon National Park visitor center, (435) 834-5322
Dog-friendly: No
Trail surface: Cement
Land status: National park

Nearest town: Bryce City
Other trail users: Hikers
Maps: www.nps.gov/brca/planyourvisit/maps.htm
Special considerations: The cement path can become icy during the fall, winter, and spring.
Other: It's approximately a few hundred feet to the overlook.
Supplies to take: Camera, tripod, camera batteries, headlamp with extra batteries, and layers of clothing. The temperature can change quite quickly in higher elevations.

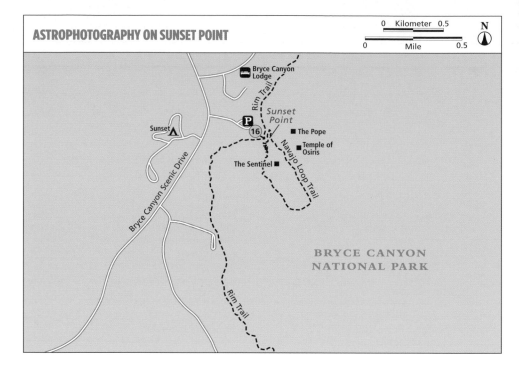

FINDING THE TRAILHEAD

From Tropic head west on UT 12 for 7.4 miles. Turn left onto UT 63 and drive another 2.6 miles to Bryce Canyon National Park. Once you have passed the entrance gate, drive another 2.3 miles to the turn for Sunset Point. Turn left and drive 0.2 mile to the trailhead.

Sunset Point GPS: N37 37.366' / W 112 09.978'

THE ADVENTURE

Once parked, grab your camera gear and head out to Sunset Point. To the north is the view of Fairyland and to the south is Inspiration and Bryce Point. To the east, straight out from the viewpoint, you may see the glow of light from Tropic.

The best shots for hoodoos in the canyon are either Fairyland or Bryce Point. During the summer, the arm of the Milky Way will stretch overhead. In late spring, it will be lower on the eastern horizon toward Tropic. Whichever direction you choose, it will be incredible with hoodoos glowing under starlight or moonlight.

> ### Other Opportunities to Enjoy the Night Sky
> **PARK RANGER-LED EVENTS**
> During spring, summer, and fall, the park offers star parties. These evening events highlight the night sky found within the park and offer the opportunity to look through a telescope at deep space objects such as nebulae, galaxies, star clusters, and more. For more information on the timing of these events, visit www.nps.gov/zion/planyourvisit/calendar.htm.

CEDAR BREAKS
NATIONAL MONUMENT

Location: 4730 S. Hwy. 148, Brian Head, UT 84719
Cost: $
Dark Sky designation: 2017

Contact: Cedar Breaks National Monument visitor center, (435) 586-0787, ext. 4040
Land status: National monument
Maps: www.nps.gov/cebr/planyourvisit/maps.htm

THIS HIGH ALPINE MONUMENT SURROUNDED BY DIXIE NATIONAL FOREST has everything you would expect, from vast meadows filled with wildflowers in the summer to towering conifers, sweeping vistas, grazing mule deer, the occasional black bear, and open views to myriad stars. Set at 10,000 feet, daytime temperatures are cool even in the summer months. In winter the monument is covered in snow.

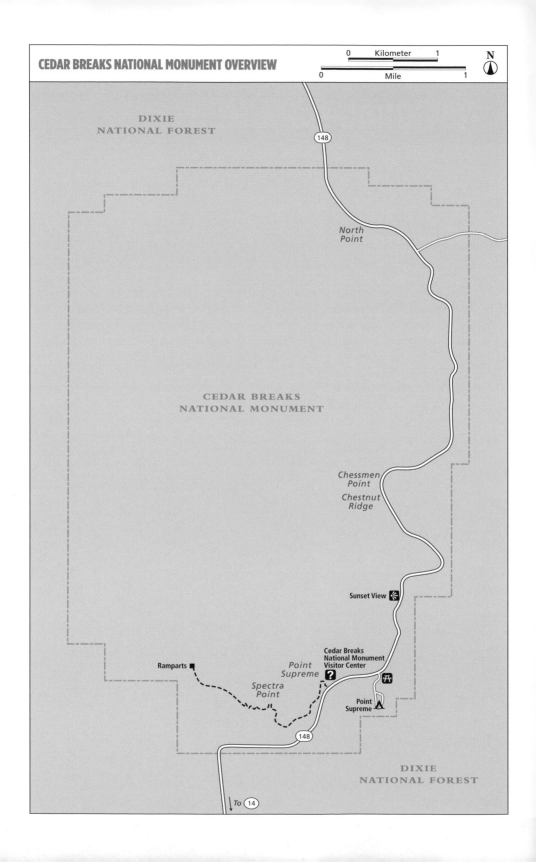

0   Kilometer   1

0   Mile   1

N

DIXIE
NATIONAL FOREST

148

*North
Point*

CEDAR BREAKS
NATIONAL MONUMENT

*Chessmen
Point*

*Chestnut
Ridge*

Sunset View

Cedar Breaks
National Monument
Visitor Center

Ramparts

*Point
Supreme*

*Spectra
Point*

Point
Supreme

148

DIXIE
NATIONAL FOREST

To 14

The real showstopper for this park is the view over the rim. Imagine a giant Creamsicle melting down from the rim onto the slopes below, leaving behind colors of soft orange and cream flowing over the soil and stone in the natural amphitheater. Limestone uplifted over millions of years has eroded into arches, fins, hoodoos, and spires. Most are stained orange by iron oxide pigments, while others have had the iron pigments removed by water, leaving them bleached white.

Many western national and state parks have CCC-built buildings and trails. The CCC was started as part of the New Deal, created to lift the United States out of the Great Depression and give young men a path to success through working within America's public lands.

The Hurricane Fault is found at the bottom of the slope in the valley floor. As this fault drops down, it pushes the mountainside up in elevation. Small earthquakes in this area are common. This fault poses a serious hazard for the communities in the valley below.

In the summer months, this monument is covered in wildflowers: bluebell, fireweed, columbine, cinquefoil, fleabane, and paintbrush. Steller's jays, Clark's nutcrackers, hummingbirds, and many other high alpine migratory birds can be found foraging within the trees, flowers, and meadows. Black bears, elk, mountain lions, foxes, deer, coyotes, porcupines, pikas, marmots, badgers, and many smaller mammals call the monument home.

For centuries, the Nuwuvi (Southern Paiute) people have called the Cedar Breaks area *u-map-wich*, which translates to "the place where rocks are sliding down all the time." They hunted game animals for meat and furs and escaped the summer heat within the mountains.

Established during Theodore Roosevelt's time, many of the older buildings were built by the Civilian Conservation Corps (CCC) with such skill and expertise, they have stood the test of time.

Today the monument is mostly visited by tourists wanting to see the incredible amphitheater below the rim. Campers will enjoy the cooler summer nights cozied up by the campfire. Stargazers will surely be dazzled by the dark and clear skies at night.

17. NIGHT HIKE ON SUNSET VIEW TRAIL

Wandering along this short cement path will take you through a beautiful high alpine meadow filled with wildflowers and a flurry of activity among birds and small mammals during the early morning and late evening. At night, everything gets pretty quiet, and a stillness returns to the meadow.

Activity: Night hike
Adventure rating: 1
Start: Cedar Breaks picnic area
Distance: 1.32 miles out and back
Elevation gain: 35 feet
Difficulty: Easy
Hiking time: About 45 minutes
Best seasons: Summer
Timing: Any time of the night; 1 hour after sunset
Fees and permits: $
Contact: Cedar Breaks National Monument visitor center, (435) 586-0787, ext. 4040
Dog-friendly: No
Trail surface: Cement

Land status: National monument
Nearest town: Panguitch
Other trail users: None
Maps: www.nps.gov/cebr/planyourvisit/maps.htm
Special considerations: The hike is wheelchair accessible.
Other: If you are sensitive to altitude sickness, bear in mind that you will be near 10,000 feet in elevation. If you experience any symptoms, move down in elevation immediately.
Supplies to take: Water, headlamp with extra batteries, and layers of clothing. The temperature can change quickly at higher elevations.

FINDING THE TRAILHEAD

From Parowan, head east on UT 143 for 15.1 miles to Cedar Breaks National Monument. The picnic area is a few miles into the monument on your left.
Cedar Breaks picnic area GPS: N37 36.735' / W112 49.854'

THE ADVENTURE

Once parked at the picnic area, strap on your backpack and head down the cement path toward Sunset Viewpoint. The first section of trail moves through a high alpine forest, a perfect place to take in the night sky.

> **LOOK UP**
> The arm of the Milky Way will stretch north to south overhead. Can you find the giant W shape of Cassiopeia? It will be toward the northern end of the Milky Way.

The wind through conifers is a sound I will always hold dear. It reminds me of my youth and camping in the mountains of Wyoming. The soft hoot of an owl calling out for a mate is also a sound not to be missed.

The path goes through a conifer forest in the final stretches toward Sunset Viewpoint. Once on the viewpoint, you can see the light from Cedar City down in the valley. The skyglow from this community lights up the amphitheater even during the night.

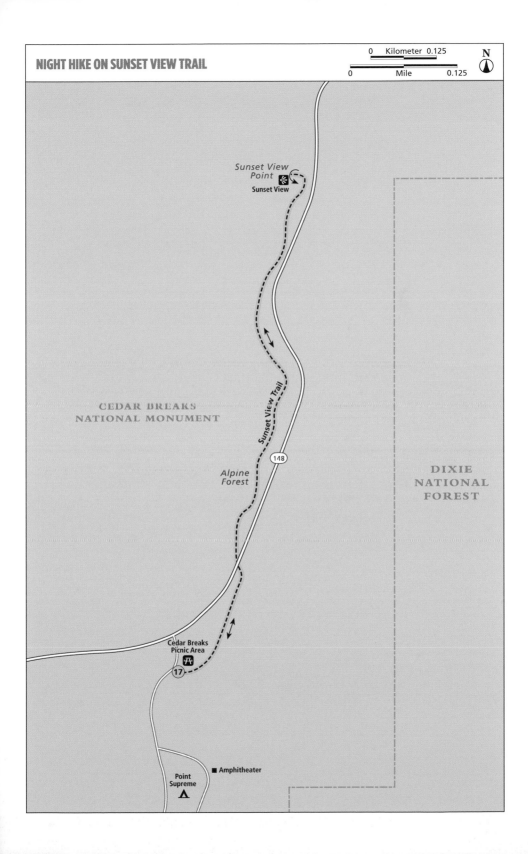

NIGHT HIKE ON SUNSET VIEW TRAIL

0   Kilometer 0.125

0   Mile   0.125

N

Sunset View
Point
Sunset View

CEDAR BREAKS
NATIONAL MONUMENT

Sunset View Trail

148

Alpine
Forest

DIXIE
NATIONAL
FOREST

Cedar Breaks
Picnic Area

17

Point
Supreme

Amphitheater

Being out at night forces you to use senses not relied on as much these days. Stop for a moment and shut off your light. Our eyes shift to using rods more than cones, removing color from our vision and moving into gray-scale. Every twig snap sounds like a large predator moving toward you. Every animal sound sets your heart aflutter. Take a moment and listen for any sounds, feel the emotions running through your body, smell the air, look around, and never forget you are by nature a preda-tor. Our fear of night is a cultural chain worth breaking. You may hear a coyote howling, an owl calling, or a small mammal scurrying around through the brush—all fascinating nighttime sounds.

LOOK UP
Find the brightest star in the summer sky, Vega. After a star is formed, the leftover bits collide into each other, forming planets. The Kepler space telescope observed a disk of matter around Vega, revealing a solar system being created.

MILES AND DIRECTIONS

0.0 Start from the picnic area parking.

0.15 Cross UT 148.

0.26 Conifer forest begins.

0.66 Reach Sunset Viewpoint and your turnaround spot.

1.32 Arrive back at the parking area.

In the winter, conifers flood sugars into the needles of the tree to keep the cells from freezing.

18. ASTROPHOTOGRAPHY ON CHESSMEN POINT

An icon of Cedar Breaks, Chessmen Point makes a wonderful location for astrophotography. Set just below the ridge is an amphitheater lined with hoodoos looking much like chess pieces with a row of conifers in front. On a quarter moon night, the amphitheater is lit up just enough to see the foreground in all of its beauty, without it looking like daylight.

Activity: Astrophotography
Adventure rating: 1
Start: Chessmen Point
Distance: 0.7 mile out and back
Elevation gain: 1 foot
Difficulty: Easy
Trip time: 1–2 hours
Best seasons: Summer
Timing: Several days after the full moon to the half moon; 1 hour after sunset
Fees and permits: $
Contact: Cedar Breaks National Monument visitor center, (435) 586-0787, ext. 4040
Dog-friendly: No
Trail surface: Cement
Land status: National monument

Nearest town: Panguitch
Other trail users: Hikers, sightseers
Maps: www.nps.gov/cebr/planyourvisit/maps.htm
Special considerations: The viewpoint is wheelchair accessible.
Other: If you are sensitive to altitude sickness, bear in mind that you will be near 10,000 feet in elevation. If you experience any symptoms, move down in elevation immediately.
Supplies to take: Water, headlamp with extra batteries, camera equipment, extra camera batteries, and layers of clothing. The temperature can change quickly at higher elevations.

FINDING THE TRAILHEAD
From Parowan, head east on UT 143 for 15.1 miles to Cedar Breaks National Monument. Chessmen Point is a few miles into the monument on your right.
Chessmen Point GPS: N37 37.841' / W112 49.955'

THE ADVENTURE
Hike the short distance out to Chessmen Point. Set up your camera equipment on the point. To the northwest are all the chessmen-shaped hoodoos. Directly in front is Cedar City. To the left is Sunset Point. From the parking lot, you can get some beautiful shots of the firs from below, stretching up to the stars.

Other Opportunities to Enjoy the Night Sky
PARK RANGER–LED EVENTS
During summer, the park offers star parties. These evening events highlight the night sky found within the park and offer the opportunity to look through a telescope at deep space objects such as nebulae, galaxies, star clusters, and more. For more information on the timing of these events, visit www.nps.gov/cebr/planyourvisit/calendar.htm.

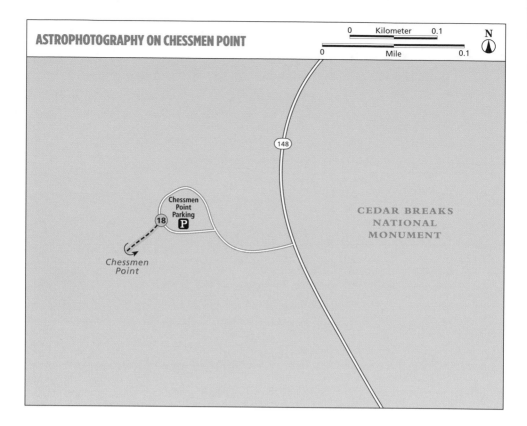

ASTROPHOTOGRAPHY ON CHESSMEN POINT

148

Chessmen
Point
Parking

18

Chessmen
Point

CEDAR BREAKS
NATIONAL
MONUMENT

0   Kilometer   0.1

0   Mile   0.1

N

I have also had a wonderful time taking photos of the tops of the firs with the stars and planets behind them. Just about everywhere you look at night in this dark sky place, the sky is filled with pinpoints of light. Photos of the meadow at night are equally mind-blowing, as are photos of the lower slopes of the amphitheater.

SOUTH-CENTRAL UTAH

FROM THE HIGH MOUNTAINS OF THE FISHLAKE NATIONAL FOREST to the low desert of the Colorado Plateau, south-central Utah is an incredible place to explore and recreate. Grand Staircase Escalante National Monument covers the majority of this area, which is known for its staggering beauty, tight slot canyons, and scenic vistas around every bend. A massive amount of sedimentary rock, which has been tilted upward on one side, forming a white spine rising upward from north to south along the eastern side of this region, is found in Capitol Reef National Park.

The entire region is part of the Colorado Plateau desert, a landscape that has been lifting upward for millions of years, causing all the rivers within it to become entrenched as they meander through deep canyons on their way to the ocean. Glen Canyon Dam was built to store water, creating the massive reservoir named Lake Powell.

Archaic people traveled through this area following megafauna south after the last ice age. On occasion, their spearheads have been found, as well as other tools. This region is also where the Ancestral Puebloan and Fremont peoples' territories crossed. Pictograph and petroglyph panels from both indigenous groups can be found throughout the region. Both used the area for hunting and foraging. Along the Utah-Arizona border, Nuwuvi (Southern Paiute) people live on their reservation, staying close to Kanab Creek, a sacred site.

South-central Utah has long drawn explorers to this foreboding landscape—explorers seeking solitude, resources, or precious metals. In the late 1800s, many settlers passed through this region headed to California, or moved into the area to start ranching and growing crops along the riverways, establishing small communities. Today some communities that rely on tourism dollars have grown, while those that do not have the infrastructure to support large-scale tourism remain small.

This area is still explored frequently by those seeking to challenge their skills, escape the cities for a remote landscape, or just get away for the weekend. Many of my favorite remote vehicle routes are within this region of Utah.

CAPITOL REEF NATIONAL PARK

Location: 52 W. Headquarters Dr., Torrey, UT 84775
Cost: $$
Dark Sky designation: 2015

Contact: Capitol Reef National Park visitor center, (435) 425-3791
Land status: National park
Maps: www.nps.gov/care/planyourvisit/maps.htm

A NEARLY 100-MILE-LONG SPINE OF ROCK stretching from north to south through south-central Utah seems to be emerging from the desert floor. This rocky spine, called the Waterpocket Fold, is a classic example of a monocline. Formed an estimated 60 million years ago when a fault shifted in the area, the west side of the fold shifted upward, sending the east side of the rock layer downward. The erosional forces of water and weathering continue to wear away at this lanky monocline, leaving behind arches, twisted

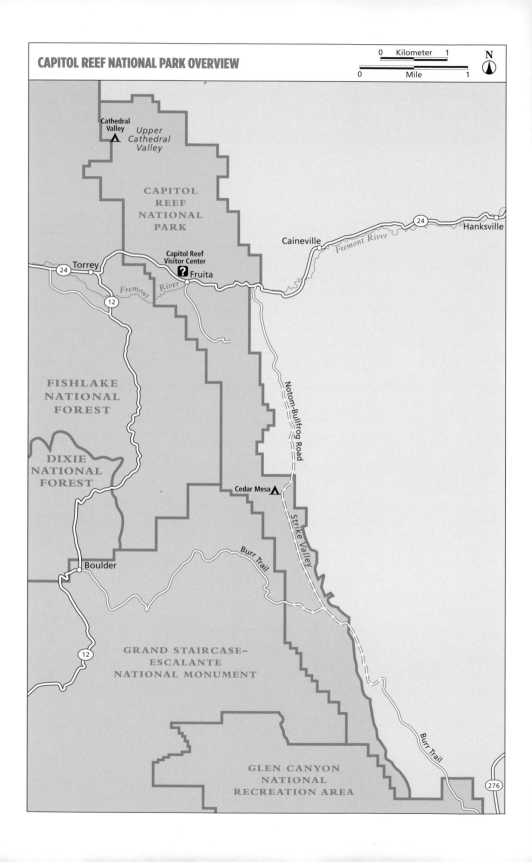

0 Kilometer 1

0   Mile   1

N

Cathedral
Valley

Upper
Cathedral
Valley

CAPITOL
REEF
NATIONAL
PARK

Caineville

Hanksville

24

Fremont River

Torrey

24

Capitol Reef
Visitor Center

Fruita

Fremont   River

12

FISHLAKE
NATIONAL
FOREST

Notom-Bullfrog Road

DIXIE
NATIONAL
FOREST

Cedar Mesa

Strike Valley

Boulder

Burr Trail

GRAND STAIRCASE–
ESCALANTE
NATIONAL MONUMENT

12

Burr Trail

GLEN CANYON
NATIONAL
RECREATION AREA

276

canyons, spires, hoodoos, domes, solitary monoliths, massive cliffs, and beautiful slot canyons. Exploring this one park alone would take a lifetime.

The hunting and foraging Fremont people traveled through this landscape, leaving behind petroglyphs and pictographs alluding to ancient ways of life. Many of the Fremont people were nomadic in lifestyle, following prey animals through their migratory patterns.

The lesson of the danger of the flash floods was a harsh one for the early settlers of the area. Elijah Culter Behunin's homestead was mostly destroyed by flash flooding, leaving only his small brick house behind, which still stands today. The orchards of Fruita, a small community of settlers that used to live in the canyon, used the patterns of water moving through the area in the Fremont River to create irrigation for the orchards. These orchards are still producing today and offer visitors the chance to pick fruit in the fall each year.

Flash flood danger still exists for those who choose to recreate in this massive park. Be mindful of the weather when traveling in slot canyons or the backcountry. If precipitation is predicted anywhere nearby, your route may fill with slick mud pits, slippery roads, or raging rivers of debris and water filling the narrow slot canyons. Due to the remote nature of the landscape and harsh environmental conditions, with little to no cellular service, be prepared to self-rescue on any adventure.

Today this rugged landscape is home to desert bighorn sheep, mule deer, mountain lions, several species of amphibians and reptiles, many bird species, many native species of fish, and around ninety species of plants. Giant Fremont cottonwood, pinyon, juniper, bristlecone pine, and many other shrubs fill in the canyons and valleys.

> Giant ponderosa pines stretch skyward from small pockets shaded from sunlight most of the day or in the higher elevations of the park. These trees are a sign of a more temperate environment in the not-so-distant past.

The National Park Service preserves the natural resources found throughout the park boundaries, including natural darkness. With the lands to the south and north of the park being public lands as well, the backcountry sites within this park provide stellar views of the Milky Way Galaxy and the universe beyond.

19. DRIVE TO CEDAR MESA BACKCOUNTRY CAMPGROUND

With nothing but public lands north and south of this campground, to say the night sky is dark is an understatement. It is truly one of the darkest sites I have ever camped in. Faint meteors were visible all night long. Midsummer days are pretty hot in this low-elevation campground; however, the nights are perfect for stargazing.

Activity: Scenic drive to backcountry camping
Adventure rating: 2
Start: Capitol Reef National Park visitor center
Distance: 60.5 miles out and back
Elevation gain: 107 feet
Difficulty: Moderate
Trip time: 2 days
Best seasons: Late spring, summer, and early fall
Timing: Any time of the month
Fees and permits: $$; campsites are first-come, first-served, free.
Contact: Capitol Reef National Park visitor center, (435) 425-3791
Dog-friendly: No
Road surface: Sand and dirt
Land status: National park
Nearest town: Torrey
Other road users: Bicyclists
Maps: www.nps.gov/care/planyourvisit/maps.htm

Special considerations: If the roads are wet or precipitation is forecast, do not do this trip. Due to the nature of the dirt, the road can become slick and form mud pits that will easily stop your progress. There are only five sites available in this campground; leave early to secure a site.
Other: Have all the supplies to walk out if necessary. If your vehicle becomes disabled, you will need to self-rescue. Bring all necessary vehicle emergency supplies (e.g., spare tire, jack, tire iron, shovel, track for getting out of deep sand, extra fluids, extra fuel).
Supplies to take: Plenty of water, food, camping gear, emergency backpack ready to go for self-rescue, night sky map, headlamp with extra batteries

FINDING THE VISITOR CENTER
Begin this trip with a quick pop into Torrey for any necessary supplies, then head east on UT 24 for 10.7 miles to the Capitol Reef visitor center.
Cedar Mesa Campground GPS: N38 00.425' / W111 05.023'

THE ADVENTURE
Inquire at the visitor center about camping at Cedar Mesa Campground. They should know if the campground has been busy or not and the condition of the road leading to it.

Once you are ready to head out, head east along UT 24 toward Fruita. In just under a mile, you will come to the Fruita schoolhouse. A quick peek inside the window reveals what the schoolhouse looked like for the few families living in Fruita. After this stop, head down the road, noting the apple orchards on both sides of the road.

There are many orchards in Fruita. You can pick apples in the fall months; inquire at the visitor center for details.

On the north side of the road, just over a mile from the visitor center, is the stop for a short hike to a Fremont petroglyph panel. The panel depicts anthropomorphs with the trapezoidal bodies and elaborate dressing typically known to be created by the Fremont.

About 6 miles from the visitor center, the Behunin Cabin still stands. This single-room cabin was once home to the Behunin family of eleven souls. It's a quick stop for a momentary ponder on what life must have been like for early settlers in this foreign desert landscape.

> Flooding destroyed much of this homestead, which resulted in the Behunin family leaving the area to look for a more hospitable site to live.

Nine miles from the visitor center, the Notom-Bullfrog Road heads south. Turn onto the road and follow it toward the Cedar Mesa Campground.

For the next 14 miles, you will pass many trailheads leading into the various slot canyons within the Waterpocket Fold. Exploring many of these canyons requires technical canyoneering skills and specialized equipment.

About 23 miles in, you will drive through the Sandy Ranch, where the landscape suddenly turns green from the agriculture and irrigation on the ranch. This is private property; please respect the owner's property rights and stay off the ranch.

At just over 30 miles, you should see the campground on the west side of the road. Drive in and pick out your site. If you have the energy, Red Canyon is a wonderful 3-mile round-trip hike up a wash into the tilted layers of the Waterpocket Fold.

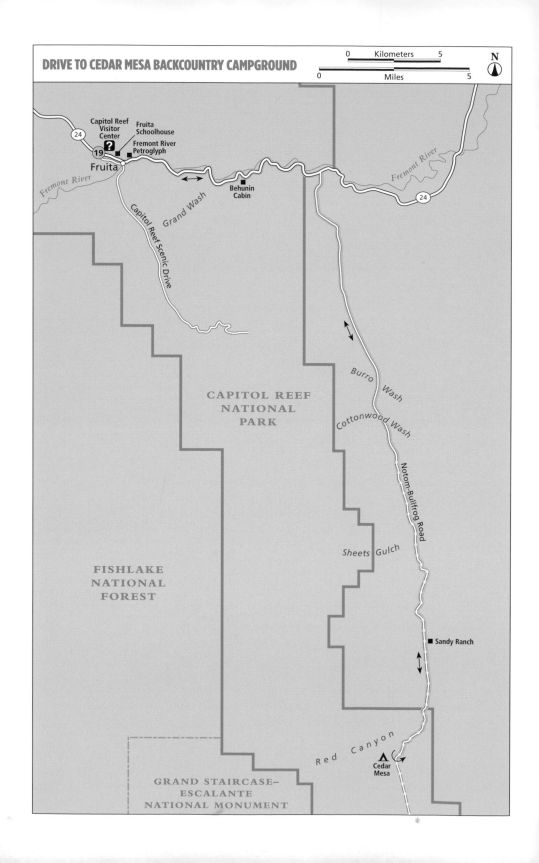

DRIVE TO CEDAR MESA BACKCOUNTRY CAMPGROUND

0 Kilometers 5
0 Miles 5

N

Capitol Reef Visitor Center
Fruita Schoolhouse
24
19
Fruita
Fremont River Petroglyph
Fremont River
Behunin Cabin
Fremont River
24

Capitol Reef Scenic Drive
Grand Wash

CAPITOL REEF NATIONAL PARK

Burro Wash
Cottonwood Wash
Notom-Bullfrog Road

Sheets Gulch

FISHLAKE NATIONAL FOREST

Sandy Ranch

Red Canyon
Cedar Mesa

GRAND STAIRCASE–
ESCALANTE
NATIONAL MONUMENT

Being out in the desert alone for several nights in a row helps reset your circadian rhythms to the natural beat of the sun, moon, and stars. This reset will bring you back to the rhythms our ancestors knew well.

If you listen carefully, you may hear an owl hoot, a coyote call, a bat using echolocation, or a common nighthawk feeding. Sleeping underneath a star-filled sky deep in the desert restores the soul.

MILES AND DIRECTIONS

0.0 Start at the Capitol Reef visitor center.

0.8 Stop at the Fruita schoolhouse.

1.14 Take the petroglyph hike to stretch your legs.

5.94 Stop at the Behunin Cabin.

9.05 Junction with Notom-Bullfrog Road; turn right (south) off UT 24 onto this road.

22.9 The Sandy Ranch is on both sides of the road.

30.25 Reach Cedar Mesa Campground. Return the way you came.

60.5 Arrive back at the visitor center.

LOOK UP

At night, pull out your night sky map. How many constellations can you identify? Which ones are always in the night sky year-round? Circumpolar stars rotate around Polaris, our North Star. They never fully set below the horizon.

20. ASTROPHOTOGRAPHY IN CATHEDRAL VALLEY

The massive monoliths within Cathedral Valley rise over 500 feet from the desert floor. The soft Entrada Sandstone seems to melt down the sides like flowing mud. In the mid-1800s, John C. Frémont's expedition moved through the Upper Cathedral Valley when they became lost in the desert. An artist by the name of Solomon Carvalho created an engraving of the scene with these monoliths in it.

While in the Upper Valley, I tried to see if I could make out any light pollution in the sky. There were only two faint domes of light that I could see in the direction of Castle Dale, north of the area. My photographs revealed an incredibly dark night sky, definitely a Bortle scale Class 2 site.

Activity: Astrophotography
Adventure rating: 2
Start: Junction of UT 72 and FR 212
Distance: 34.58 miles out and back
Elevation loss: 2,554 feet
Difficulty: Moderate
Trip time: 2 days
Best seasons: Late spring, summer, and early fall
Timing: Any time of the month
Fees and permits: Free
Contact: Capitol Reef National Park visitor center, (435) 425-3791
Dog-friendly: No
Trail surface: Sand, rock, and dirt
Land status: National park
Nearest town: Torrey
Other road users: None
Maps: www.nps.gov/care/planyourvisit/maps.htm
Special considerations: If the roads are wet or precipitation is forecast, do not do this trip. Due to the nature of the dirt, the roads can become slick and form mud pits that will easily stop your progress. There are only a few sites available at Cathedral Valley Campground; leave early to secure a site. You will need a 4x4 vehicle for this adventure.
Other: Have all the supplies to walk out if necessary. If your vehicle becomes disabled, you will need to self-rescue. Bring all necessary vehicle emergency supplies (e.g., spare tire, jack, tire iron, shovel, track for getting out of deep sand, tow rope, extra fluids, extra fuel). Camping at Cathedral Valley Campground is advisable for this adventure.
Supplies to take: Plenty of water, food, camping gear, emergency backpack ready to go for self-rescue, night sky map, camera gear, tripod, extra camera batteries, and headlamp with extra batteries.

FINDING THE ROAD

Take exit 86 off I-70 onto UT 76 toward Fremont for 2.6 miles. Turn right onto UT 72 headed south for another 16.3 miles. FR 212 will be on your left.
Upper Cathedral Valley monoliths trailhead GPS: N38 29.278' / W111 21.194'

THE ADVENTURE

From UT 72, turn east onto FR 212 and follow the road for about 5 miles. At this point you can see Geyser Peak on the southwest side of the road; FR 212 wraps around it. Just past 6 miles is the junction with FR 206; turn left onto this road.

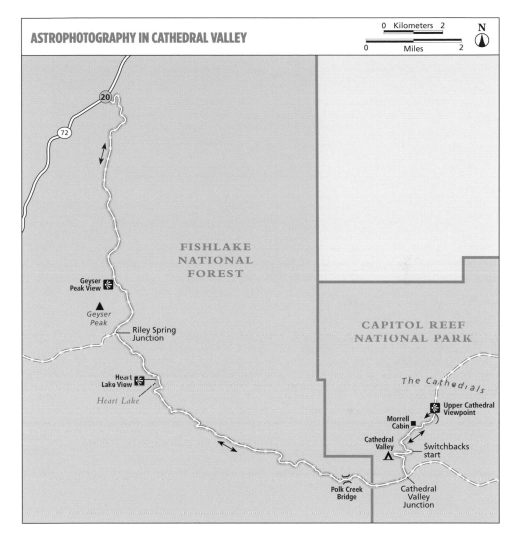

0 Kilometers 2

0 Miles 2

N

FISHLAKE
NATIONAL
FOREST

Geyser
Peak View

Geyser
Peak

Riley Spring
Junction

Heart
Lake View

Heart Lake

CAPITOL REEF
NATIONAL PARK

The Cathedrals

Upper Cathedral
Viewpoint

Morrell
Cabin

Cathedral
Valley

Switchbacks
start

Polk Creek
Bridge

Cathedral
Valley
Junction

Just under 8 miles, you can see Heart Lake on the south side of the road. After passing the lake, keep a watch out for FR 022; turn left onto this road and follow it down the mountain. There will be several opportunities to view the Upper Cathedral Valley area from above.

The road follows Polk Creek to the border of Capitol Reef National Park. Once inside the park, the road becomes extremely rough and rocky; take your time through this section. Watch for a sign for the Cathedral Valley Campground. Turn left once you see it. You are now on one side of the Cathedral Valley Road.

If you plan to camp, pop into the campground and set up camp while you wait for it to get dark. You may even want to head down into Upper Cathedral Valley before the sun sets. The Morrell Cabin is down in the valley. It is a short 0.25-mile hike to the cabin. Please do not take anything from this

> Morrell Cabin and its corrals were used seasonally by local ranchers for respite from the desert while moving livestock.

nationally registered historic site.

Continue up the road for another mile to your photography site for the night. The monoliths will be obvious, as they are massive. Find your favorite vantage point and set up for the night.

Caution: Only serious off-roaders should continue forward on either side of the Cathedral Valley Road. The road is notorious for deep pits of fine sand that a vehicle can easily get stuck in. It is nearly 100 miles to the nearest community. If you do decide to continue, please travel with several vehicles so that you can help each other if one of you becomes stuck. This road is remote! You will most likely not see anyone else until you are closer to UT 24.

LOOK UP

Once you are finished, head back to the campground or all the way back to UT 72. If you decide to camp, spend some time stargazing. You are in one of the darkest areas in the United States. Do you see the shape of a backwards question mark made of stars? If so, you've found Leo. Leo, and Virgo just below, have many galaxy clusters within their constellation boundaries.

MILES AND DIRECTIONS

0.0   Start at the junction of UT 72 and FR 212.

4.85   Geyser Peak view.

6.27   Junction of FR 212 and FR 206; turn left onto FR 206.

7.74   Heart Lake view.

8.08   Junction of FR 206 and FR 022; turn left onto FR 022.

13.4   Cross the bridge over Polk Creek.

14.88   Junction with Upper Cathedral Valley road; turn left.

15.19   Junction for Cathedral Valley Campground.

15.31   Switchbacks drop down to Upper Cathedral Valley.

16.64   Morrell Cabin.

17.29   Upper Cathedral Valley monoliths. Return the way you came.

34.58   Arrive back at the UT 72/FR 212 junction.

GOBLIN VALLEY STATE PARK

Location: PO Box 637, Green River, UT 84525
Cost: $$
Dark Sky designation: 2016

Contact: Goblin Valley State Park visitor center, (435) 275-4584
Land status: State park
Maps: https://stateparks.utah.gov/parks/goblin-valley/map/

GOBLIN VALLEY STATE PARK IS TRULY A PLACE THAT STIRS the imagination! The shapes and forms of the goblins themselves are mind-blowing. Some of the hoodoos sit on narrow bases that appear barely able to support their weight. The three sculptors of this magical landscape were water flowing over the surface, removing any loose sediment; ice expanding, popping apart the stone and allowing water to move the remnants; and wind smoothing out the harder sandstone left behind. These tenacious sculptors have been working for millions of years to create the masterpieces we see today.

Valley of the Goblins at night is surreal. Every shape looks like it could come alive at any moment. Seeing the goblins mixed with pinpoints of stars can leave you feeling like you've entered a science fiction world or unknown planet. Ranging in size from giant boulders to the size of a semitruck, weaving your way through the goblins transports you to another world. The valley is about 2 miles long and 1 mile wide, giving ample space to play.

Goblin Valley has long been known to the indigenous people who have lived in this area for over a thousand years. Within the San Rafael Swell, an anticline just west of Goblin Valley, Fremont pictograph and petroglyph panels can be found. This landscape was used as hunting grounds and migration routes for these nomadic people.

Today the park draws people from around the world to behold the unique geological features it was named after. The park has a variety of hiking and mountain biking trails. There are yurts and a campground to stay the night, which provide shade and shelter from the hot summer sun and windstorms that roll through this area.

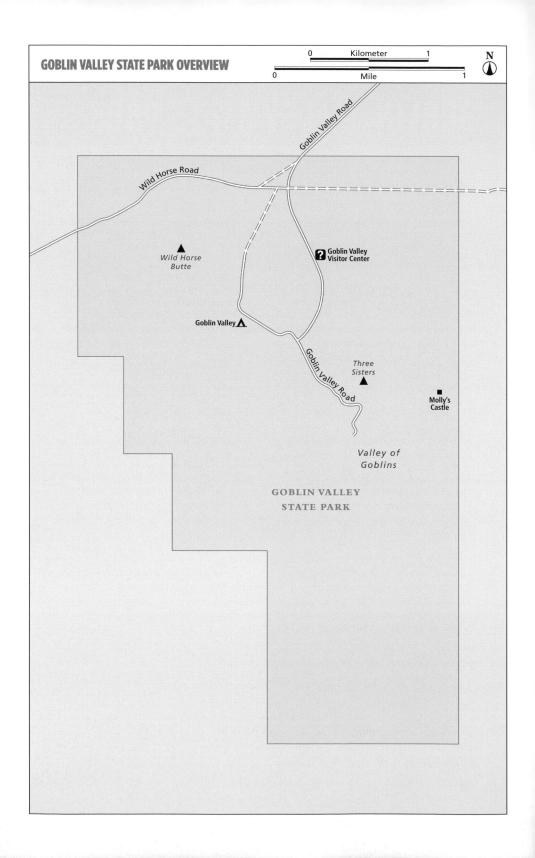

21. HIDE-AND-SEEK IN VALLEY OF THE GOBLINS

The goblins in Valley of the Goblins are just begging for exploration. The shapes and quantity of hoodoos are astounding. These massive goblin-shaped stones are made of Entrada Sandstone, a rather soft sandstone. They are best observed from the ground, and climbing on them is not recommended. When in the valley at night, the goblins seem to take on a whole other shape with the long shadows from moonlight. It feels otherworldly and foreign. The stars shine above like little lanterns.

Activity: Hide-and-seek
Adventure rating: 1
Start: Goblin Valley observation point
Distance: 0.4 mile out and back
Elevation loss: 20 feet
Difficulty: Easy
Trip time: About 1 hour
Best seasons: Late spring, summer, and early fall
Timing: From the half moon to the full moon
Fees and permits: $$
Trail contact: Goblin Valley State Park visitor center, (435) 275-4584
Dog-friendly: No
Trail surface: Rock and dirt
Land status: State park
Nearest town: Hanksville

Other trail users: Hikers
Maps: https://stateparks.utah.gov/parks/goblin-valley/map/
Special considerations: Define your area limits while it is still daylight, and discuss what to do if someone feels lost or scared. The "teams of two" system is highly recommended for all children.
Other: Give each person a whistle in case there are issues, someone gets lost, or to signal the round is over. The day-use areas close at 10 p.m.
Supplies to take: Headlamp with extra batteries, whistle, layers of clothing, two red lanterns (to remain on the picnic tables at the observation area)

FINDING THE TRAILHEAD

From Green River follow I-70 west for 10.5 miles to UT 24. Take exit 149 off the interstate and travel 24.2 miles south to Temple Mountain Road. Turn right onto Temple Mountain Road and drive another 12.8 miles. Turn left onto Goblin Valley Road and travel another 6.9 miles to the park entrance station. Goblin Valley Overlook is another mile beyond the entrance station.
Valley of Goblins observation point GPS: N38 33.817' / W110 41.977'

THE ADVENTURE

For this adventure, I think a daytime investigation of the area is a grand idea. This will give children the opportunity to see the formations in the daylight so their silhouette isn't frightening at night. It's also a good time to define boundaries, talk about safety, and discuss what to do if someone gets lost or feels scared.

> The goblins are formed by water freezing and thawing, with wind adding the finishing touches to smooth them out.

At twilight, return to Valley of the Goblins and set up for your adventure. Place two red lanterns on the tables at the observation point as a base for anyone who feels scared or once everyone is called to return from a round. Establish some simple rules. Here are a few I would suggest:

> Red and green light is easy on our eyes at night and allows us to still see the stars.

1. If you get lost, stop moving and hold still. Blow your whistle so an adult will know to come find you.

2. Whistles are only to be used if lost or for a quick signal that the round is over.

3. Stay within the boundary established at all times (keep your boundary relatively small to keep everyone within hearing range and sight of the lanterns' glow).

4. Do not climb on the goblins.

5. Listen for the signal that the round is over, and return immediately once you hear it.

6. With children, play in teams of two, with the agreement that teams are not to separate under any circumstances.

7. For those found, have them return to the lanterns until the next round begins.

8. Take time to enjoy the night sky while out among the goblins at night.

9. All restroom breaks need to be taken in a bathroom. With many people enjoying this area each day, please help keep it clean and free of the smell of urine.

10. Have fun!

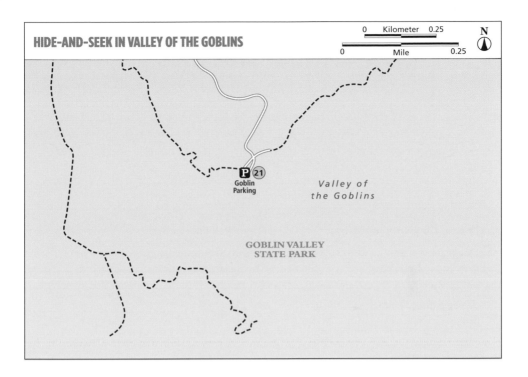

0   Kilometer   0.25

0   Mile   0.25

N

P 21
Goblin
Parking

*Valley of
the Goblins*

GOBLIN VALLEY
STATE PARK

After a few rounds, come back together and check in with everyone to see how they are feeling. Take a moment to look up and remember the beauty of the night found in the stars.

22. ASTROPHOTOGRAPHY OF THREE SISTERS

The Three Sisters is a distinct Entrada Sandstone formation with three spires at the top that look like people in hats. This feature has long been a favorite for astrophotographers. In the summer months, the Milky Way can be seen behind it, making it a wonderful foreground object for astrophotography.

Activity: Astrophotography
Adventure rating: 1
Start: Goblin Valley observation point
Distance: 0.78 mile out and back
Elevation loss: 35 feet
Difficulty: Easy
Trip time: 1–2 hours
Best seasons: Any season
Timing: A few days after the full moon to a few days after the new moon
Fees and permits: $$
Trail contact: Goblin Valley State Park visitor center, (435) 275-4584
Dog-friendly: No
Trail surface: Rock and dirt

Land status: State park
Nearest town: Hanksville
Other trail users: None
Maps: https://stateparks.utah.gov/parks/goblin-valley/map/
Special considerations: The ground is uneven and may be ice covered during the winter. Check conditions before proceeding.
Other: The first 0.25 mile follow the road; if you see a car coming, exit the pavement or make your presence known by light.
Supplies to take: Headlamp with extra batteries, clothing in layers, camera gear, extra camera battery, tripod, water, and night sky map

FINDING THE TRAILHEAD

From Green River follow I-70 west for 10.5 miles to UT 24. Take exit 149 off the interstate and travel 24.2 miles south to Temple Mountain Road. Turn right onto Temple Mountain Road and drive another 12.8 miles. Turn left onto Goblin Valley Road and travel another 6.9 miles to the park entrance station. Goblin Valley Overlook is another mile beyond the entrance station.
Valley of Goblins observation point GPS: N38 33.817' / W110 41.977'

THE ADVENTURE

From the observation point parking area, head back up the road you just drove in on. After about 0.25 mile, you will see the trail to the Three Sisters to the right and their silhouette in the distance. Head up the trail to the feature and set up for the night. Please remember to stick to the trail in your travels and place your tripod on hard surfaces.

MILES AND DIRECTIONS

0.0 Start from the observation point parking area.

0.25 Junction with Three Sisters trail off Goblin Valley Road; turn right.

0.39 Three Sisters formation and end of the trail. Return the way you came.

0.78 Arrive back at the parking area.

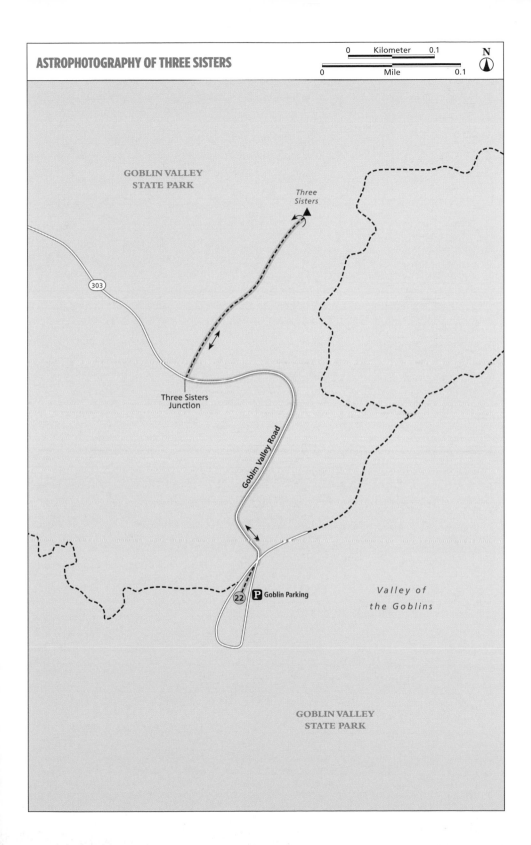

0   Kilometer   0.1

0   Mile   0.1

N

GOBLIN VALLEY
STATE PARK

Three
Sisters

303

Three Sisters
Junction

Goblin Valley Road

22   P Goblin Parking

Valley of
the Goblins

GOBLIN VALLEY
STATE PARK

HONORABLE MENTIONS

TORREY

Location: 100 N. 75 E., Torrey, UT 84775
Dark Sky designation: 2018
Contact: Torrey Town Hall, (435) 425-3600

Land status: Municipal
Maps: https://torreyutah.gov/contact-us/
GPS: N38 18.027' / W111 25.775'

The town of Torrey is located just west of Capitol Reef National Park. This small community is mostly agriculture farms and livestock ranches. Torrey is often seen as the gateway to Capitol Reef National Park. There are a few tourism businesses based in Torrey and many options for overnight lodging if you'd like a bed to sleep on.

RAINBOW BRIDGE NATIONAL MONUMENT

Location: 691 Scenic View Dr., Page, AZ 86040
Cost: $$
Dark Sky designation: 2018

Contact: Glen Canyon National Recreation Area, (928) 608-6200
Land status: National monument
Maps: www.nps.gov/rabr/planyourvisit/maps.htm

Rainbow Bridge is one of the most massive natural bridges known to exist in the United States. From its base to its highest point is about 295 feet, making it taller than the Statue of Liberty. The bridge spans 275 feet across a dry wash that fills with water when the rains come. Today the riverbed only fills during flash floods or when Lake Powell overflows, which doesn't happen very often. You can hire a guide who will take you by boat to the monument, then it is a simple, approximately 1-mile hike to the bridge.

This area was considered sacred to the Ancestral Puebloan people and still is to the local indigenous peoples, especially the Nuwuvi (Southern Paiute) and Diné Bikéyah (Navajo). To be in this place is an honor; please visit with respect.

HELPER

Location: 58 S. Main St., Helper, UT 84526
Dark Sky designation: 2020
Contact: Helper city offices, (435) 472-5391, www.helpercity.net/dark-sky

Land Status: Town
Maps: www.udot.utah.gov/main_old/uconowner.gf?n=89563328019277451
GPS: N39 41.048' / W110 51.278'

This small community snuggled up to ore-rich shales met by massive, sandstone cliffs became a dark sky community early in 2020. An area long visited by indigenous people for hunting of bighorn sheep, the nearby Nine Mile Canyon holds many petroglyph panels created by the Fremont people.

The name Helper was adopted by the community, as it is well known as a train hub for the Pacific Railroad. A Helper car of a train is an extra engine used to help trains move over the nearby Soldier Summit while pulling a heavy load.

SOUTHEAST UTAH

SOUTHEASTERN UTAH IS THE HEART OF THE COLORADO PLATEAU and boasts one of the darkest night sky viewing areas in the United States. The first International Dark Sky Park certification, in 2007, was given to Natural Bridges National Monument, in the heart of this region. This designation was followed by four other parks in the area gaining International Dark Sky Park certification: Hovenweep, Canyonlands, and Arches National Parks, as well as Dead Horse Point State Park. The majority of this region is public land, with only the light from fossil fuel extraction impacting the night sky.

The landscape of southeastern Utah is one of high mesas, towering buttes, striking spires, deep canyons, silty rivers, and verdant valleys. Most of the mountains in this region were formed under the pressure of rising magma that did not breach the surface. Instead, the magma pushed the layers of sedimentary rock upward, creating the laccolithic mountain ranges of the La Sal, Abajo, and Henry Mountains. River canyons hundreds of feet deep stand as a testament to the power of water within the desert as the Green and Colorado Rivers, entrenched in their path, move toward the ocean. The Colorado River Delta ends in the Gulf of California.

These remote, rugged landscapes were pathways for ancient peoples, who left their marks on the canyon walls and alcoves. Approximately 2,000 years ago, the Ancestral Puebloan people occupied much of southeastern Utah. They led farming lives, growing maize, beans, and squash, and keeping domesticated animals within their dwelling grounds. The Puebloans lived in villages year-round and continued their forager-hunter lifeway. Many pictographs, petroglyphs, cliff and tower dwellings, kivas, and toolmaking sites remain in the Four Corners area. Pottery, as well as many comfortable household wares, were created by the Puebloan people and can be seen in museums in the Four Corners region. A massive drought developed across Utah approximately 1,300 years ago. It's believed that many of the Puebloan and Fremont people moved southward in search of resources, some returning to forager-hunter lifeways. Many of the current indigenous peoples of the Four Corners area claim the Ancestral Puebloans as their ancestors.

The first record of a European being in Utah is by the Rivera Expedition. In 1765, Juan María Antonio Rivera led an expedition to map the land north of Santa Fe, New Mexico. After the Spanish expedition, the area was a haven for outlaws, ranchers, and miners seeking their fortunes. Today there are still pockets of mines, farms, and ranches; however, most of the region relies heavily on tourism dollars to thrive.

Today these lands are a mecca for outdoor recreation, from the tame to the extreme. When backpacking, mountain biking, paddling, or river rafting along the mesas or in the canyons of the backcountry, the night sky is so vibrant. The myriad stars overwhelm the usually visible constellations, making it more challenging to pick out familiar shapes. Meteors can be spotted streaking across the sky almost every night. If you happen to be on a mesa top in early spring or late fall, zodiacal light shines high in the night sky. With most of the parks in this area registering as Class 2–3 sites on the Bortle scale,

you are bound to see sights in the night sky that you have never seen before. The truly dark skies of her hometown of Moab ignited a lifelong love of starry skies for the photographer of this guide, Bettymaya Foott, a love that drives her work to protect natural darkness.

CANYONLANDS NATIONAL PARK

Location: UT 313, Moab, UT 84532
Dark Sky designation: 2015
Contact: Canyonlands National Park visitor center, (435) 719-2313

Land status: National park
Maps: www.nps.gov/cany/ planyourvisit/maps.htm

INTERSECTED BY THE GREEN RIVER AND THE COLORADO RIVER, Canyonlands National Park is divided into three sections with unique defining characteristics: the mazelike canyons in the Maze District, the high mesa views down into the canyons in the Island in the Sky District, and the needlelike hoodoos among the canyons in the Needles District.

This landscape has long been visited by humans, from the Archaic people following the migration patterns of megafauna to the Ancestral Puebloan people moving along the waterways, leaving behind petroglyph and pictograph panels along the way. Granaries, structures, and dwellings can still be found among the landscapes of Canyonlands National Park. Current-day indigenous peoples of the Four Corners area return to their ancestral lands for ceremonies and the traditional gathering of resources.

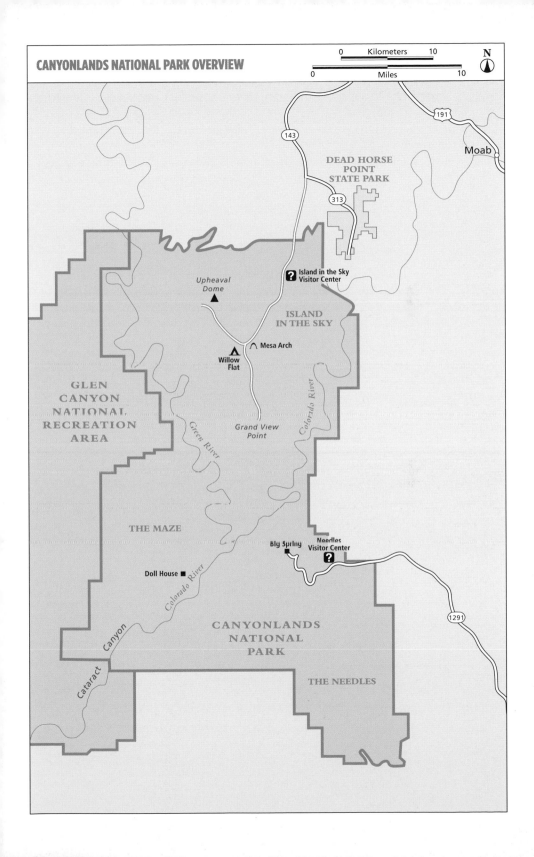

The myriad deep canyons provided a reprieve from the pursuit of law officers for outlaws familiar with the landscape. Ranchers used the upper-elevation meadows for grazing cattle and sheep. Historic explorers traveled the deep canyons of the Green and Colorado Rivers. John Wesley Powell, Denis Julien, and Antoine Robidoux explored much of the length of the Green River. They paddled over ancient seabeds where the ocean came and retreated nearly thirty times, creating the massive Paradox Formation below the riverbed.

The geology of this park spans hundreds of millions of years, back to a time when dinosaurs roamed the land along what is today the Kayenta Formation. Ancient beach sands form the White Rim, a white sandstone found along the White Rim Road, which is popular among mountain bikers, backpackers, and 4x4 drivers. The massive needle-shaped hoodoos found within the Needles District, formed by an ancient beach or sand-bar on an inland sea turning to stone through pressure and cementation, have captivated backpackers and hikers for generations.

Today much of this landscape is home to desert bighorn sheep, mule deer, mountain lions, black bears, coyotes, foxes, jackrabbits, scorpions, bats, lizards, toads, birds, and many small rodents. The ample water in the riverways allows for a wide variety of life to exist in these remote areas of the Colorado Plateau. Remember, you are only passing through their home. Travel with care, and pack out everything you bring in.

23. BACKPACKING IN CHESLER PARK

Strapping a backpack full of all that you will need for several days to your back and heading out into the backcountry of the Needles District gives you a sense of empowerment. Travel through this rugged landscape is not for the faint of heart. Desert travel often takes you up sandstone hills, then down into deep, dry canyons and back out again. Walking through deep sand for a portion of the trek tests your tenacity to get to your destination. You will be walking ancient pathways through gorgeous landscapes with modern gear. It is always enlightening to think of what it would have taken to make this same trek before all this fancy gear was created.

Activity: Backpacking
Adventure rating: 2
Start: Elephant Hill trailhead
Distance: 8.0 miles out and back
Elevation gain: 495 feet
Difficulty: Difficult
Trip time: 3 days (3.5-hour hike in and 3-hour hike out)
Best seasons: Late spring, summer, and early fall
Timing: Any time
Fees and permits: $$; www.nps.gov/cany/planyourvisit/backcountrypermits.htm
Contact: Needles District visitor center, (435) 259-4711
Dog-friendly: No
Trail surface: Dirt and rock
Land status: National park
Nearest town: Monticello
Other trail users: None

Maps: www.nps.gov/cany/planyourvisit/maps.htm
Special considerations: You will need to pack personal waste bags and carry them out. All water needed must be packed in. You cannot rely on water being available in the canyons.
Other: This hike is in a remote area of the park. You may or may not see others, depending on the season and weather.
Supplies to take: Tent, backpack, sleeping bag, pad, layers of lightweight clothing, two pairs of socks, sturdy shoes, water and food for 4 days (extra for emergencies), first-aid kit, wag bags, salty snacks, electrolytes, and any personal items you are willing to carry

FINDING THE TRAILHEAD

From Main Street in Moab, head south along US 191 for approximately 40 miles. Turn right onto UT 211 and travel through beautiful Indian Creek headed toward Canyonlands National Park's Needles District. Travel for another 37.2 miles. Turn left on FR 2444 and travel 0.3 mile, then turn right toward Elephant Hill and drive another 0.2 mile. Turn right once more onto the dirt road headed toward Elephant Hill trailhead. You arrive at the trailhead in about 2.7 miles.
Elephant Hill trailhead GPS: N38 08.504' / W109 49.622'

THE ADVENTURE

Once you've checked in at the Needles visitor center backcountry office, drive to the Elephant Hill trailhead. Pack up your backpack with the heaviest items in the bottom. Be sure enough water is easily accessible for the hike in. Take a minute before heading

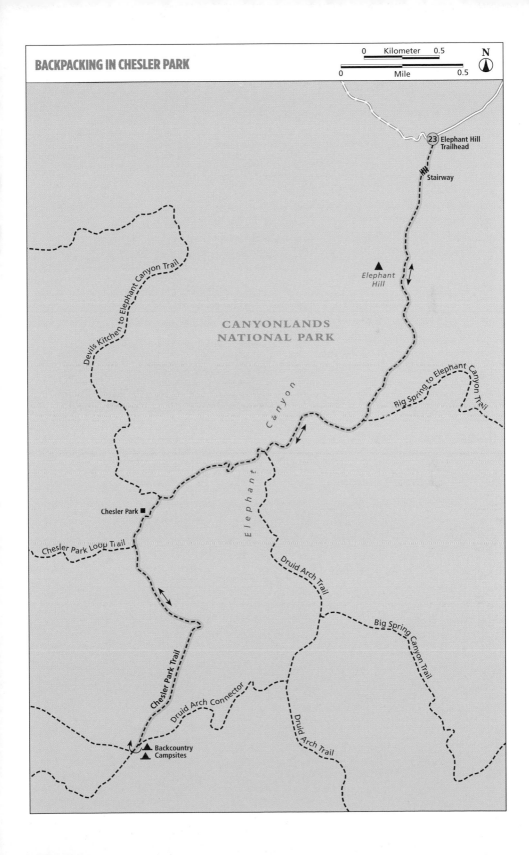

BACKPACKING IN CHESLER PARK

0   Kilometer   0.5

0   Mile   0.5

N

23 Elephant Hill
Trailhead

Stairway

Elephant
Hill

CANYONLANDS
NATIONAL PARK

Devils Kitchen to Elephant Canyon Trail

Big Spring to Elephant Canyon Trail

Canyon

Elephant

Chesler Park ■

Chesler Park Loop Trail

Druid Arch Trail

Big Spring Canyon Trail

Chesler Park Trail

Druid Arch Connector

Druid Arch Trail

▲ Backcountry
▲ Campsites

up the trail to adjust your straps so the weight of the pack is over your hips. Once you are ready, head out.

The route climbs quickly at the beginning to get you up to an upper plateau, where you will walk past Elephant Hill on a gentle grade. After the plateau, the trail climbs again before dropping down into Elephant Canyon.

The trail up and out of Elephant Canyon is a steep haul. Take your time and watch your footing. With some sections of exposure, a slip could mean injury. Once out of the canyon, you will cross another plateau, heading toward a cliff of banded Cedar Mesa Sandstone. The trail crosses the plateau toward the cliff.

> Shade is crucial to cool down during a hot summer day for all wild animals. Follow their lead and take a shade break.

After the plateau, you will climb up another section of steep trail to the edge of Chesler Park, which is a massive open area surrounded by the famous hoodoos of the Needles District. The trail heads south and across the majority of Chesler Park before leading to the backcountry campsites.

Find your campsite and set up camp. Welcome to an incredibly dark place. If you time your trip to the new moon, you will be amazed at how much you can see. With no communities to the south, the night sky will steal the show. If you time it to a meteor shower, you are sure to never forget the trip!

There are lots of offshoot trails to explore during the daytime from Chesler Park. Check out all the options before heading back out.

LOOK UP
In a dark night sky, you can often see a few meteors per night.

MILES AND DIRECTIONS

0.0 Start at the Elephant Hill trailhead.

0.16 Stairway to upper plateau.

0.58 Reach Elephant Hill.

1.34 Junction with Elephant Canyon Trail; stay on the trail to Chesler Park.

1.73 Drop down into Elephant Canyon.

2.61 Junction with Devil's Kitchen Trail; stay on the trail to Chesler Park.

2.76 North end of Chesler Park.

2.89 Junction with Chesler Park West Trail; stay on Chesler Park Trail headed south toward the backcountry campsites.

4.0 Chesler Park backcountry sites. Return the way you came once your stay is over.

8.0 Arrive back at the trailhead.

24. ASTROPHOTOGRAPHY OF MESA ARCH

Mesa Arch is an iconic landscape feature found in the Island of the Sky District of Canyonlands National Park. It is a favorite among photographers visiting the area for sunrise shots, as you can frame the rising sun inside of the arch, reducing the sunlight to rays of light. In the early summer months, you can get the arch of the Milky Way over the arch during the early morning hours, then stay for the iconic sunrise photo. Don't forget to capture Washer Woman Arch in the picture, which can be seen in the distance toward the La Sal Mountains.

Activity: Astrophotography
Adventure rating: 1
Start: Mesa Arch trailhead
Distance: 0.59-mile loop
Elevation gain: 64 feet
Difficulty: Easy
Trip time: 1–2 hours
Best seasons: Any season
Timing: A few days after the full moon to a few days after the new moon
Fees and permits: $$
Contact: Island in the Sky visitor center, (435) 259-4712
Dog-friendly: No

Trail surface: Dirt and rock
Land status: National park
Nearest town: Moab
Other trail users: None
Maps: www.nps.gov/cany/ planyourvisit/maps.htm
Special considerations: When it gets close to sunrise, many photographers flock to the area.
Other: Please stay off the arch; a fall here would mean death.
Supplies to take: Camera gear, extra camera body, tripod, layers of clothing, headlamp with extra batteries

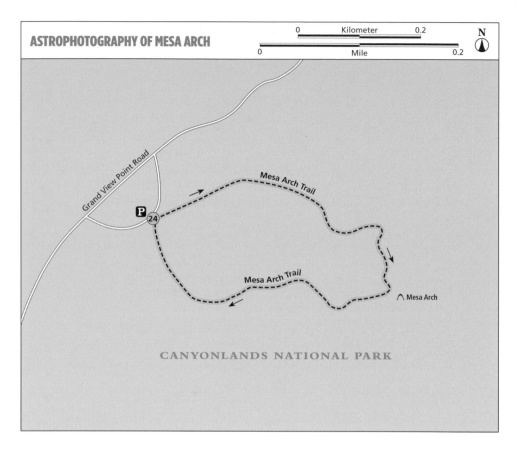

FINDING THE TRAILHEAD

From Main Street in Moab, head north on US 191 to the junction with UT 313 for approximately 11 miles. Turn left on US 313 and climb up to the mesa top for another 14.6 miles; at this point US 313 will turn left, but you will need to continue straight ahead toward Canyonlands National Park. Continue straight for 14.6 miles and watch for the Mesa Arch trailhead on your left.

Mesa Arch trailhead GPS: N38 23.350' / W109 52.071'

THE ADVENTURE

After leaving the parking lot, head east toward the La Sal Mountains. It's a quick 0.3 mile to the arch. Set up your camera gear and enjoy the shoot. After your photography session, finish out the other side of the loop trail to see some of the best examples of biological soil crust I have ever seen.

MILES AND DIRECTIONS

0.0 Start at the Mesa Arch trailhead; bear left.

0.31 Mesa Arch.

0.59 Arrive back at the trailhead.

25. WHITEWATER RAFTING CATARACT CANYON

The thrill of rafting down the mighty Colorado River, through rapids that John Wesley Powell and his expedition traveled, is guaranteed to form a lifelong memory. The sound of the rapids reverberates off the canyon walls long before you see them, building the anticipation that will get your heart pumping. Side hikes off the river lead you to ancient dwellings of the Ancestral Puebloan people.

Activity: Whitewater rafting
Adventure rating: 1
Start: Your guide will determine the meeting site.
Distance: 95.44 miles one way
Elevation loss: 247 feet
Difficulty: Difficult
Trip time: 3 days and 2 nights
Best seasons: Any season
Timing: Any time
Fees and permits: $$$+
Contact: www.nps.gov/cany/ planyourvisit/guidedtrips.htm
Dog-friendly: No
River surface: Whitewater
Land status: National park
Nearest town: Moab
Other canyon users: Paddlers, hikers, backpackers

Maps: www.nps.gov/cany/ planyourvisit/maps.htm
Special considerations: Hire a guide for this trip! A quick trip down the river requires a motor. Going on your own requires a permit, which is difficult to acquire, and technical whitewater skills. Bring a Colorado River guide to follow along with your trip progress.
Other: Be sure to bring long layers of clothing for the hot summer months to save your skin from sunburn. Bring electrolytes to help replenish salts lost from sweating.
Supplies to take: Camera, headlamp with extra batteries, sleeping bag and pad, tent, layers of clothing, and any personal items

THE ADVENTURE

The first 47 miles of this trip is a flatwater section of the Colorado River. You will travel around the gooseneck that can be seen from Dead Horse Point State Park.

If you look up to the top of the mesa to the south of the tip of the gooseneck, you may be able to make out tiny silhouettes of people up at the park.

> This gooseneck will at some point be abandoned as the river breaks through its narrow neck.

As you continue down the river, the canyon walls will begin to rise. It is not uncommon to see blue herons along the side of the river, waiting for a luckless fish to swim by. Keep watch for peregrine falcons and golden eagles along the cliff faces.

At about 19 miles, a popular archaeology site called Coffee Pot Ruin is a common stop. This is an Ancestral Puebloan dwelling site. As you investigate this area, you will see many pictographs and petroglyphs. Please remember to be respectful of this site and not touch anything or take anything you may find.

> Keep a watch out for giant stick nests in trees or boulders. Herons create rookeries, or nesting colonies.

> The painted hands were made by artists putting paint in their mouth and then blowing it out quickly with their hand between their mouth and the wall.

At about 31 miles, the massive wash of Indian Creek Canyon will appear on river left. Much farther upcanyon, Indian Creek is a world-class climbing area with massive cliffs filled with cracks that draw climbers from all over the world.

Next you will meander around The Loop, a 5-mile twist and turn in the river. At about 47 miles, you will come to the confluence of the Green and Colorado Rivers.

At mile 51, Red Lake Canyon is visible to the left. The giant sandbar on river left is often a campsite for these quick trips down the river. Across the river and above the cliffs are the hoodoos of the Doll House in Canyonlands National Park's Maze District. You are now officially in Cataract Canyon.

At mile 52, Brown Betty Rapid is your first whitewater of the trip. From here, you will pass a continuous series of rapids and campsites. Rapids 13–18 are all part of Mile Long Rapid.

There are several inscriptions from past expeditions through the canyon, most dating to the late 1800s through the early 1900s. Ask your guides if they can show you any. After rapid 20, Ben Hurt Rapid, the river gets real exciting! You are about to go through

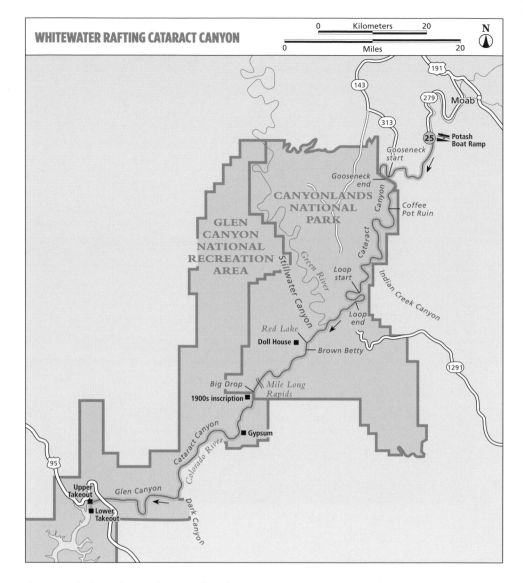

three rapids that John Wesley Powell and company portaged (carried their boats and gear by land) around. Hold on tight.

Big Drop I, II, and III are the most technical and intense whitewater rapids in Cataract Canyon. While your guides scout the rapid, if you are able, walk the bank and look for fossils. Here you can find shell and crinoid fossils, signs of an ancient seabed.

Your second campsite will most likely be somewhere after these rapids. This will be the night to sleep outside in the open if you are comfortable with that. You are now deep into the wilderness of Canyonlands National Park. It is truly one of the darkest nights I've spent out. There is just something special about sleeping under the stars. When you wake during the night, notice how much the stars have shifted in the sky.

At about mile 67 you will arrive at Gypsum Canyon, the technical start of Lake Powell. Lower Cataract Canyon has sparse campsites, depending on the current level of the reservoir. Most of the lower section is now rapid free due to the reservoir's creation. The next almost 30 river miles are flatwater sections with high cliff walls. I found myself gazing up at all the different formations at the tops.

Your journey will come to an end at one of two boat ramps in the Hite area of Lake Powell. Don't forget to tip your guides! They work hard for your comfort.

MILES AND DIRECTIONS

0.0   Start at the Potash boat ramp.

10.64 Beginning of gooseneck.

14.22 End of gooseneck.

18.92 Coffee Pot Ruin.

30.82 Indian Creek Canyon.

36.17 Start of The Loop.

42.31 End of The Loop.

47.3   Confluence of Green and Colorado Rivers.

50.76 Red Lake Canyon.

51.56 Brown Betty Rapid.

60.29 Mile Long Rapids.

61.47 Big Drop Rapids.

61.81 Kolb Expedition inscription from 1911.

67.06 Gypsum Canyon.

80.78 Dark Canyon.

95.44 Arrive at the Hite takeout.

Other Opportunities to Enjoy the Night Sky
PARK RANGER-LED EVENTS
During summer, the park offers star parties. These evening events highlight the night sky found within the park and offer the opportunity to look through a telescope at deep space objects such as nebulae, galaxies, star clusters, and more. For more information on the timing of these events, visit www.nps.gov/cany/planyourvisit/calendar.htm.

ARCHES NATIONAL PARK

Location: US 191, Moab, UT 84532
Dark Sky designation: 2019
Contact: Arches National Park visitor center, (435) 719-2299

Land status: National park
Maps: www.nps.gov/arch/planyourvisit/maps.htm

WITH OVER 2,000 ARCHES WITHIN ITS BOUNDARIES, Arches National Park is one of the most sought-out national parks in the southwestern United States. The story of erosion and weathering of iron-rich sandstone can be seen throughout this beautiful park. From the patterned holes seen within the lofty cliff faces to the massive arches, towering fins, salt valleys, and tafone scenes engraved in sandstone walls, it was all created through the erosional forces of water, ice, and wind.

Entrada Sandstone towers over much of the desert shrub landscape. Sights include the fins and hoodoos of Devil's Garden, the deep maze of Fiery Furnace, the mammoth arches within the Windows District, the standing spires of the Garden of Eden, and the

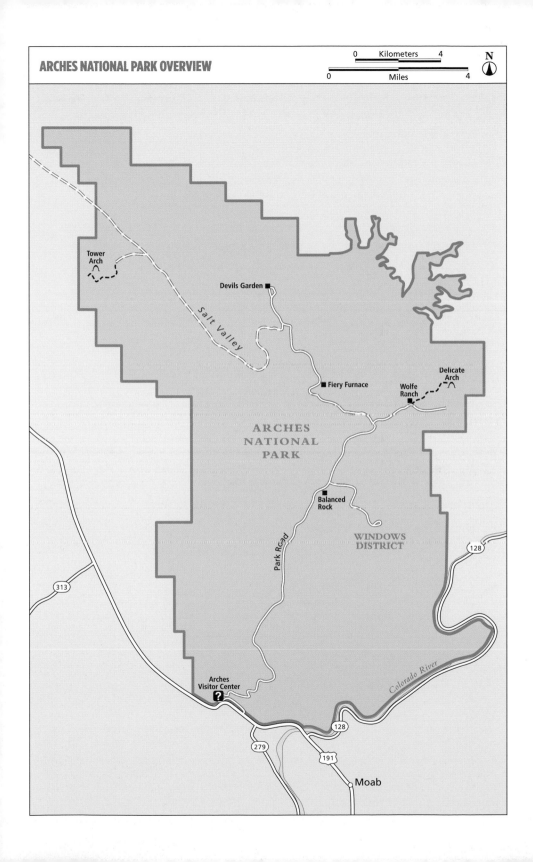

hoodoos and balanced rocks in the Balanced Rock area. Striking views can be seen wherever you explore.

The park is home to bighorn sheep, mule deer, mountain lions, bobcats, coyotes, kit foxes, golden eagles, peregrine falcons, reptiles, amphibians, and many smaller mammals. You are most likely to encounter kit foxes, ground squirrels, cottontail rabbits, and many species of lizards.

The landscape is covered in blackbrush, four-winged saltbush, sagebrush, and juniper trees. Towering cottonwood trees grow along Courthouse Wash. Biological soil crust covers the landscape, providing support for surrounding plants by fixing nitrogen in the soil, storing water, and providing shelter from wind for new seedlings.

You may find petroglyphs dating back to the Ancestral Puebloan people that once called this landscape home. They used this land to hunt and forage. Today the descendants of these people still forage these lands, gathering plants for ceremonial purposes. Many of the current Pueblo people consider them their ancestors. Near Wolfe Ranch is a petroglyph panel created by the Núu-agha-tuvu-pu (Ute) people of this area. Archaeologists draw attention to the horse within the scene, as horses were not common in the region until after the Spanish explorers arrived.

A few settlers moved into the Arches area in the late 1800s. Most did not stay for very long. The Wolfe family lived at the ranch from the late 1890s to 1913. They raised cattle and grew food to survive.

Whether you spend your day climbing the spires in the Garden of Eden, hiking across ancient dunes to view the world-famous Delicate Arch, exploring the labyrinth of Fiery Furnace, or peering through the windows in the Windows District, you are sure to create memories that will last a lifetime.

26. NIGHT HIKE TO DELICATE ARCH

Iconic Delicate Arch graces many Utah license plates and souvenirs throughout Utah. This massive sandstone arch is sculpted out of the rock, and the fact that it remains despite the erosion of the rest of the layer it was surrounded by seems unfathomable. The scene's backdrop is the gorgeous La Sal Mountains, which rise nearly 13,000 feet above sea level. The moon will rise from behind these mountains, adding to the spectacle.

Activity: Night hike
Adventure rating: 2
Start: Delicate Arch trailhead
Distance: 3.06 miles out and back
Elevation gain: 586 feet
Difficulty: Difficult
Hiking time: About 2 hours
Best seasons: Any season
Timing: 1 hour before sunset
Fees and permits: $$$
Trail contacts: Arches National Park visitor center, (435) 719-2299
Dog-friendly: No
Trail surface: Dirt and rock
Land status: National park

Nearest town: Moab
Other trail users: Hikers only
Maps: www.nps.gov/arch/planyourvisit/maps.htm
Special considerations: You will need a lot of water due to exposure to the sun and the difficulty of the hike.
Other: Please do not leave pets in your vehicle. It is much too hot most of the year for an animal to survive a hot vehicle.
Supplies to take: Drinking water, salty snacks, camera, lenses, and headlamp with extra batteries

FINDING THE TRAILHEAD

Head north along US 191 until you reach the turn for Arches National Park approximately 4.6 miles from Main Street. Turn right onto Arches Scenic Drive. Travel 12.13 miles along Arches Scenic Drive to Delicate Arch Road. Turn right onto Delicate Arch Road and drive for a short 1.2 miles to main trailhead parking.
Delicate Arch trailhead GPS: N38 44.139' / W109 31.232'

THE ADVENTURE

The hike begins through the flat of Wolfe Ranch. There are a few historic buildings here for your viewing. The Wolfe family lived on this ranch in the late 1800s. Six members of the family lived in this one-room cabin. They raised cattle and sheep on the native vegetation in the surrounding Salt Wash Valley.

Take a moment on the bridge crossing to look down along the stream banks. Often you will see American bullfrogs along the waterline. These invasive species often feed on native tadpoles for food.

After walking through the valley, you will climb a massive sandstone hill. This is the most difficult part of the hike and is fully exposed to the sun. Plan your hike accordingly. In midsummer, you may want to hike in by the full moon as well as hike out.

NIGHT HIKE TO DELICATE ARCH

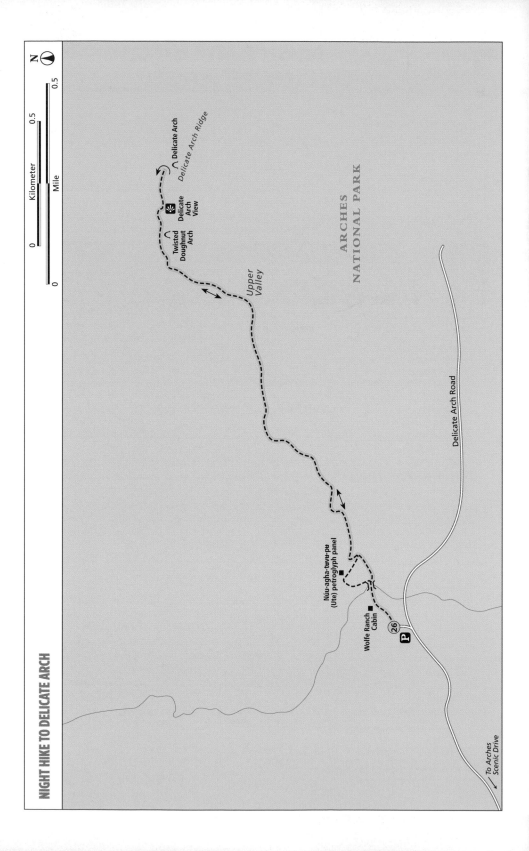

N

Kilometer
0   0.5

Mile
0   0.5

Delicate Arch
Delicate Arch Ridge

Delicate Arch View

Twisted Doughnut Arch

Upper Valley

ARCHES NATIONAL PARK

Núu-agha-tʉvʉ-pʉ (Ute) petroglyph panel

Wolfe Ranch Cabin

26

P

Delicate Arch Road

To Arches Scenic Drive

The first known photograph of Delicate Arch was taken by Flora Stanley in 1906 while living at Wolfe Ranch with her father, brother, and husband. The camera was a gift from her husband to help ease her discomfort at living at the ranch.

Once you crest the top of this massive lithic dune, you will move through an upper sandstone canyon. This area is sand covered with a few plants. On the far side of the canyon is the final climb up a cutout sandstone stairway and path. If you encounter ice on this stretch, please do not proceed. The exposure is too great to risk a fall.

After completing the carved pathway, you will come around the corner to the full view of Delicate Arch and the sandstone bowl below. Please do not attempt to go into the bowl. Many people have died trying to access the bowl.

Find a nice place to kick back and eat some of the snacks you brought while watching the gorgeous sunset glow on the arch. Enjoy watching the full moon rise from behind the La Sal Mountains. The return hike provides pure moonlight washing across the sandstone, the perfect finish to a wondrous trip.

MILES AND DIRECTIONS

0.0 Start from the Delicate Arch trailhead.

0.07 Wolfe Ranch.

0.12 Cross a bridge.

0.54 Start climbing a sandstone hill.

1.03 Reach the upper valley.

1.36 Twisted Doughnut Arch.

1.45 Delicate Arch view.

1.53 Delicate Arch ridge. Retrace your steps the way you came.

3.06 Arrive back at the Delicate Arch trailhead.

> **LOOK UP**
> Do you see the C-shaped constellation next to Boötes? This is the "northern crown," or Corona Borealis.

27. ASTROPHOTOGRAPHY IN THE WINDOWS DISTRICT

With three massive windows and Double Arch nearby, astrophotography within this area of the park is stellar. It is easy to frame the perfect night sky photograph using one of the three windows. With some planning, you might be able to capture the full moon through one of the windows or get the Milky Way aligned in Turret Arch. Whatever vantage point you decide on, the photographs are sure to be filled with stars.

Activity: Astrophotography
Adventure rating: 1
Start: Windows District trailhead
Distance: 0.72-mile lollipop loop
Elevation gain: 88 feet
Difficulty: Easy
Trip time: About 25 minutes
Best seasons: Any season
Timing: 4 days after the full moon through the half moon; 1 hour after sunset
Fees and permits: $$
Contact: Arches National Park visitor center, (435) 719-2299
Dog-friendly: No
Trail surface: Dirt and rock
Land status: National park

Nearest town: Moab
Other trail users: None
Maps: www.nps.gov/arch/planyourvisit/maps.htm
Special considerations: Please stick to the trails provided to protect the biological soil crust.
Other: Do not light paint the arches. Light painting is against park regulations and will disturb other photographers. If you'd like the arch to show color, shoot with a bit of moonlight instead of on a new moon.
Supplies to take: Drinking water, salty snacks, camera, extra camera battery, tripod, and headlamp with extra batteries

FINDING THE TRAILHEAD
Head north along US 191 until you reach the turn for Arches National Park, approximately 4.6 miles from Main Street. Turn right onto Arches Scenic Drive. Travel 9.9 miles along Arches Scenic Drive to the right turn to the Windows District. In another 2.5 miles, you will arrive at the Windows trailhead.
Windows District trailhead GPS: N38 41.229' / W109 32.207'

THE ADVENTURE
The trail begins with a slight incline toward the North Window. This window is best shot from below the final set of stairs. The stairs will look as if they are leading up to a window shaped like an eye. Gorgeous shot!

Just past the North Window, you will walk around the corner and drop down a bit. A short trail branches off to the left; take that to the South Window. The South Window provides the perfect silhouette frame for photos filled with stars. Get up close to the arch for this one. If you are on the north side of the arch, you can also get distant Turret Arch in the shot on nights with a touch of moonlight.

Return to the main trail and continue south to Turret Arch. This massive arch provides the opportunity to photograph a stand-alone feature surrounded by dark skies and possibly the Milky Way during certain times of the year.

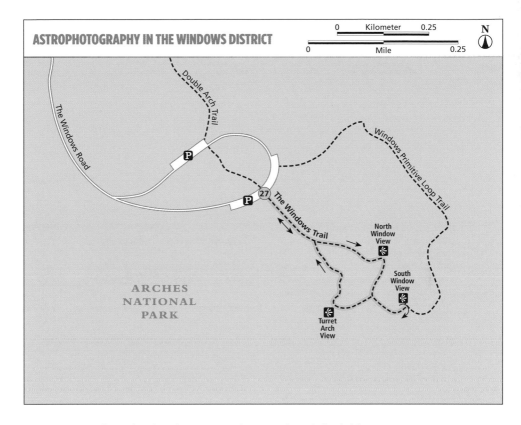

Option: Looking for the chance to make your friends look like giants? As an extra, hike over to Double Arch on the other end of the district for a photograph below a double arch on the northwest side of the Windows District. These massive arches provide the perfect blend of arches and sky for astrophotography. Take the photo from below of your friends looking up at the arches, and they will look like giants.

MILES AND DIRECTIONS

0.0 Start at the Windows District trailhead.

0.12 Reach the trail split for the loop; turn left.

0.26 North Window view.

0.31 Junction with trail to South Window; turn left.

0.36 South Window view. Return to main trail; turn left.

0.48 Turret Arch view.

0.6 Return to the trail split; turn left toward the trailhead.

0.72 Arrive back at the Windows District trailhead.

28. PLEIN-AIR PAINTING AT BALANCED ROCK

Balanced Rock features a massive stone resting on a narrow neck that slowly broadens out into a wide foot. This world-famous view makes the perfect backdrop for a night plein-air painting session. Whether you choose a new moon night or full moon night, the opportunity to paint in the quiet of night is incredible.

Activity: Plein air night painting
Adventure rating: 1
Start: Balanced Rock trailhead
Distance: None
Elevation gain: None
Difficulty: Easy
Trip time: About 1 hour
Best seasons: Spring, summer, and fall
Timing: 1 hour after sunset
Fees and permits: $$
Contact: Arches National Park visitor center, (435) 719-2299
Dog-friendly: No
Trail surface: Concrete and dirt
Land status: National park

Nearest town: Moab
Other trail users: Astrophotographers
Maps: www.nps.gov/arch/planyourvisit/maps.htm
Special considerations: Please stick to the trails provided to protect the biological soil crust.
Other: Do not light paint the arches. Light painting is against park regulations and will disturb photographers.
Supplies to take: Drinking water, painting supplies, comfortable chair, and headlamp with red or green light options

FINDING THE TRAILHEAD

Head north along US 191 until you reach the turn for Arches National Park, approximately 4.6 miles from Main Street. Turn right onto Arches Scenic Drive. Travel 9.6 miles along Arches Scenic Drive to the Balanced Rock trailhead.
Balance Rock trailhead GPS: N38 42.106' / W109 33.959'

THE ADVENTURE

Being out underneath the night sky is awe-inspiring. I often think of several of van Gogh's night paintings when I'm planning a night paint. There is something magical to capturing the essence of the night during the night—you are there under the night sky, taking it all in, connected to the universe beyond Earth.

Painting at night allows your creativity to go wild. With daylight colors no longer visible, playing with color at night is great fun. My favorite site for painting in this area is from GPS point N38 42.089' / W109 33.925'. To help keep my painting straight, I tape the paper to an artist's board ahead of time. This is easy to attach to your backpack with some rope and carabiners. This spot is close to the trailhead, so bring a chair for comfort.

Once there, set up your paint supplies before darkness hits. I even suggest sketching out the landscape. If you don't know your paint palette colors, you may also want to do a test sheet of the colors so you know what you are working with. I suggest taking a moment and writing the name of the shade next to the test sheet. Just add a small dab of each color in the order it is in your tray to paper or canvas you do not intend on using for the piece. This will help once darkness sets in.

I usually draw a basic outline and any prominent features by red light before painting. Once it is time to paint, you can turn your light to a low-intensity white (or label your paint tray as described above) so you know what color you are using. It will look very different under red light. If you have memorized your palette, you can use red or green light, which will help you see the night sky above.

Take a few moments to orient yourself to the night sky. See if you recognize any of the stars or con-stellations you can see above. It is always fun to view night sky pieces with recognizable constellations

Setting your headlamp to the lowest brightness setting will help you see the stars.

LOOK UP
Each of those pinpoints of light is a star that began its life by fusing hydrogen into helium within the core of the newly formed star, starting nuclear fusion.

Balanced rocks are rocks that seem barely balanced on the layer of stone beneath them.

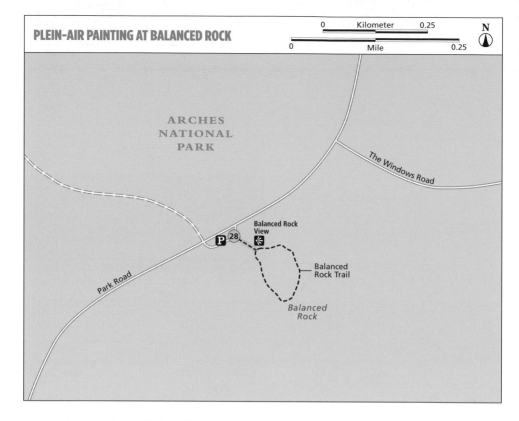

among the pinpoints of light. The easy way is to flick white paint over the sky, though, and that's perfectly acceptable.

After you have completed your painting, kick back and enjoy the night sky while it dries. In the desert, this usually doesn't take too long. Then pack up and head back to your vehicle the way you came.

Other Opportunities to Enjoy the Night Sky
PARK RANGER–LED EVENTS
During summer, the park offers star parties. These evening events highlight the night sky found within the park and offer the opportunity to look through a telescope at deep space objects such as nebulae, galaxies, star clusters, and more. For more information on the timing of these events, visit www.nps.gov/arch/planyourvisit/calendar.htm.

HOVENWEEP NATIONAL MONUMENT

Location: The entrance to this monument is difficult to find. Do not follow your GPS. Consult the national park website for detailed directions at www.nps.gov/hove/planyourvisit/directions.htm.
Dark Sky designation: 2014

Contact: Hovenweep National Monument visitor center, (970) 562-4282, ext. 5
Land status: National monument
Maps: www.nps.gov/hove/planyourvisit/maps.htm

Evidence of this area being used by hunter–forager paleolithic peoples dates back 10,000 years ago at the Cajon site. The site was used as a hunting ground.

Consisting of six different Ancestral Puebloan structural sites, Hovenweep National Monument is an excellent place to visit. More than 2,500 individuals are believed to have lived here between AD 1200 and 1300. Towers made of stone and mud mortar stand above the horizon, considered by some archaeologists to be watchtowers to protect the precious resources of those that lived here. Others theorize that they might have a celestial alignment. This mystery remains unsolved.

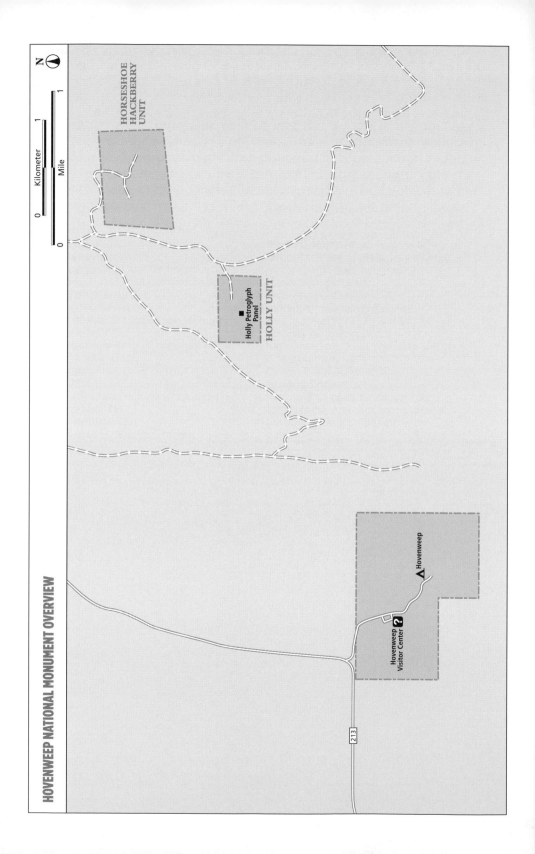

HOVENWEEP NATIONAL MONUMENT OVERVIEW

N

Kilometer
0   1

Mile
0   1

HORSESHOE
HACKBERRY
UNIT

Holly Petroglyph
Panel

HOLLY UNIT

Hovenweep
Visitor Center

Hovenweep

213

Structures were also built on giant boulders. It takes remarkable craftsmanship to create something that stands over a thousand years later. Springs were used to irrigate crops. Granaries were built under the canyon lip to store caches of food. Evidence of terracing techniques for stormwater irrigation has been discovered.

Walking along the rim today, you can hear the sound of water dripping into the pools below. Look to the east at Sleeping Ute Mountain rising from the desert floor. This mountain is sacred to many of the Four Corners peoples, who consider the Ancestral Puebloan people their ancestors. Birds are plentiful due to the fresh spring water. The occasional desert cottontail may be seen feeding on forbs. Deer, pronghorn, bobcats, coyotes, hares, birds, and many rodents call these lowlands home.

Explore the towers, structures, springs, and other areas left undisturbed throughout the monument to better understand the ancestors of the current Four Corners peoples. If you camp, sit along the rim and take in the sights, sounds, and smells. Look up and take in the night sky above. The ancient peoples that lived here looked up into this same night sky. Unfortunately, hiking after sunset is not allowed at this monument, so camping is the only way to enjoy the park at night.

29. **SOLSTICE HIKE TO HOLLY SOLSTICE MARKER**

This is a daytime hike in celebration of a celestial event. Solstice markers are fascinating to behold. The Holly solstice marker is made up of three spiral petroglyphs that are pierced by a beam of light from the side as the sun shines through a hole in the boulder on the summer solstice. Seeing this example of indigenous knowledge of the sun, moon, and seasonal cycles is incredible.

Activity: Hike
Adventure rating: 1
Start: Holly Ruin trailhead
Distance: Approximately 0.5 mile out and back
Elevation loss: 6 feet
Difficulty: Easy
Hiking time: 1.25–1.75 hours
Best seasons: Summer solstice (June 20, 21, or 22, depending on the year)
Timing: Be at the trailhead ready to roll by 10 a.m.
Dog-friendly: No
Trail surface: Dirt and sandstone
Fees and permits: Free
Contact: Hovenweep National Monument visitor center, (970) 562-4282 ext. 5
Land status: National monument

Nearest town: Cortez, CO
Other trail users: Hikers only
Maps: www.nps.gov/hove/planyourvisit/upload/HOVE_VisitorGuide-web.pdf
Special considerations: Visitors are only allowed on trails within the monument between sunrise and sunset. You will need a high-clearance vehicle to get to this trailhead. Road may be impassable when wet.
Other: Be mindful of your surroundings. This landscape is rugged, and a misstep could result in injury.
Supplies to take: Drinking water, salty snacks, trail map, camera, and binoculars

FINDING THE TRAILHEAD

Head south on US 191 until you reach UT 262 about 14.8 miles from Blanding. Turn left onto UT 262 headed east for 8.4 miles. Turn left onto Hovenweep Road and drive for another 6.7 miles. Turn right on Reservation Road and drive for another 9.4 miles. Turn left to stay on Reservation Road and continue for another 5 miles. Continue straight onto CO 213/Hovenweep Road for 0.9 mile. The visitor center will be on your right; however, continue straight ahead for another 4.07 miles. You will see a dirt road on your right; pull off and check the kiosk to be sure you are at the Holly Ruin road. Follow the dirt road for 1.85 miles to Holly Unit trailhead. Keep a watch out for the Hovenweep sign markers, which are brown painted signs with a bird symbol on them. They will help to keep you on track.
Holly Ruin trailhead GPS: N37 23.990' / W109 02.422'

THE ADVENTURE

The trail is hard-packed rock and soil and lined by a small rock border. Short junipers and pinyons provide only sparse shade. Sagebrush, rice grass, snakeweed, ephedra, and cliffrose line the trail corridor, creating a feast for the senses.

> This site is believed to be 800 years old.

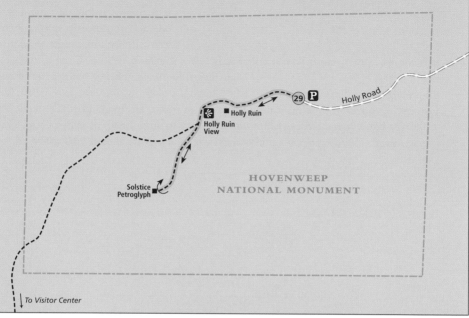

Along the way, you will come to a leaning tower built on a boulder. Incredibly, it has been standing since the 1200s. Its height is staggering. Keep your eyes open for small creeks running just past this area. This little spring was the primary water source for this site.

Continue around the canyon to the Holly tower. On your way, look for a boulder covered in desert varnish; petroglyphs cover this boulder. Holly tower allows you to get closer to the structures and see how wood was used to brace the walls and strengthen the structure.

The petroglyph overlook is the next stop and your destination for this adventure. You will be standing above the boulder in the canyon. You may need to back up a bit to see under the overhang of the boulder. Three spiral petroglyphs are what you are looking for. About 45 minutes after sunrise, a shaft of sunlight will pierce through all three petroglyphs.

> Many archaeoastronomers believe that sites such as these were an indicator of shifts in crop cultivation, markers of the passage of time.

MILES AND DIRECTIONS

0.0 Start at the Holly Ruin trailhead.

0.13 Holly tower.

0.25 Reach the solstice marker. Return the way you came.

0.5 Arrive back at the trailhead.

30. ASTROPHOTOGRAPHY AND CAMPING IN HOVENWEEP NATIONAL MONUMENT

Photographing Sleeping Ute Mountain with stars all around and possibly the Milky Way arching above is an incredible experience. You are looking at the night sky from the same place the Ancestral Puebloan people once gazed up from a thousand years earlier. The ruins in this monument have some alignment with the sun and moon at various equinox and solstice times. These indigenous people knew the patterns of the sun, moon, planets, and stars. They tracked these patterns to know when to time crops and harvest.

Activity: Astrophotography
Adventure rating: 1
Start: Hovenweep National Monument visitor center parking lot
Distance: None
Difficulty: Easy
Trip time: 1–2 hours
Best seasons: Any season
Timing: A few days after the full moon to a few days after the new moon
Dog-friendly: No
Trail surface: Pavement
Fees and permits: Free; campsites are first-come, first-served, $.
Contact: Hovenweep National Monument visitor center, (970) 562-4282, ext. 5

Land status: National monument
Nearest town: Cortez, CO
Other trail users: None
Maps: www.nps.gov/hove/planyourvisit/upload/HOVE_VisitorGuide-web.pdf
Special considerations: Visitors are only allowed on trails within the monument between sunrise and sunset. You may take photos from the campground if you are camping or from the visitor center parking lot.
Supplies to take: Camera with extra battery, tripod, headlamp with extra batteries, and layers of clothing

FINDING THE TRAILHEAD

Head south on US 191 until you reach UT 262, about 14.8 miles from Blanding. Turn left onto UT 262 headed east for 8.4 miles. Turn left onto Hovenweep Road and drive for another 6.7 miles. Turn right on Reservation Road and drive for another 9.4 miles. Turn left to stay on Reservation Road and continue for another 5 miles. Continue straight onto CO 213/Hovenweep Road for 0.9 mile. The visitor center will be on your right.
Hovenweep visitor center parking GPS: N37 23.160' / W109 04.845'

THE ADVENTURE

In Hovenweep campground, try to choose a site close to the rim of the canyon. At night, find a comfortable spot to sit or lie down. Listen to the sounds of nocturnal life. Sound travels a long way during the silence of the night. Which sounds can you identify: the sound of dripping from a spring, water running over rock, toads croaking, nocturnal rodents hunting for food, or something new and unfamiliar?

Many desert animals are active during the night to avoid the taxing heat of the day. During the day, they stay underground in cooler burrows. Nighttime food harvesting also helps keep small animals safe from predators if they are cautious.

Look up from your listening site. What new constellation and legend can you create out of the stars above? Share your new constellation and legend with your friends. This is precisely how constellations were created. Often the legends told stories of societal expectations, indicated the timing of planting or harvest of crops, or were fun warnings on the importance of being truthful. Cultures across the globe have stories associated with unique constellations. Now you have added your own to the mix.

Diné Bikéyah (Navajo) cultural traditions state that stories of the sun, moon, and stars may only be told during the winter months, November to March. Winter is seen as a time of reflection, allowing these stories to emerge.

If you are not camping, once you arrive at the visitor center, pull out your camera gear and set up. Enjoy your night of astrophotography and stargazing among these ancient landscapes. Remember that you are not allowed on the trails at night, so stick to the parking lot.

Other Opportunities to Enjoy the Night Sky
PARK RANGER–LED EVENTS
During summer, the park offers star parties. These evening events highlight the night sky found within the park and offer the opportunity to look through a telescope at deep space objects such as nebulae, galaxies, star clusters, and more. For more information on the timing of these events, visit www.nps.gov/hove/planyourvisit/calendar.htm.

NATURAL BRIDGES
NATIONAL MONUMENT

Location: The entrance to this monument is at the end of UT 275, roughly 35 miles west of Blanding along UT 95. Driving time from Blanding is roughly 45 minutes.
Dark Sky designation: 2005

Contact: Natural Bridges National Monument visitor center, (435) 692-1234, ext. 616
Land status: National monument
Maps: www.nps.gov/nabr/planyourvisit/maps.htm

NATURAL BRIDGES NATIONAL MONUMENT REMAINS one of my favorite places to enjoy the night sky. New moon nights are incredibly dark, making it hard to not stay awake all night observing the universe above. Full moon nights bring the canyon walls to life; they shine brightly, bathed in moonlight. Three bridges found in this monument are the namesake of this protected area. Natural bridges are formed by water moving

NATURAL BRIDGES NATIONAL MONUMENT OVERVIEW

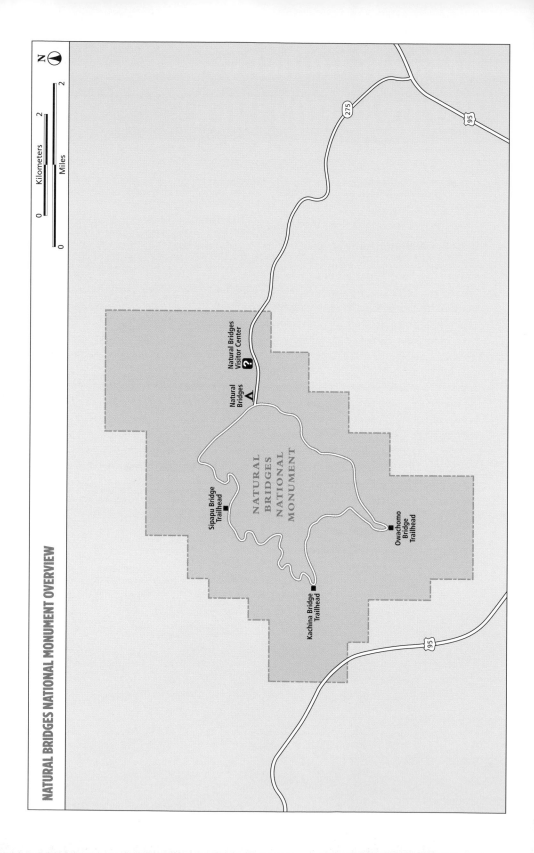

underneath sandstone, carving away the stone as it flows. After many years, only the outline of that pathway remains. White Canyon Creek was the force behind the formation of these bridges.

This monument and the land surrounding it were home to the Ancestral Puebloan people. Dwellings, granaries, pictographs, petroglyphs, kivas, and cists are found throughout this region. Some areas are so littered with potsherds and lithic scatter that you begin to understand how long these people lived here. In some areas, you can see on the sandstone walls and boulders where tools were sharpened, cages where wild turkeys were kept, springs where water was collected, stones where grains were ground into flour, and footholds cut into canyon walls. These people farmed and lived their lives within these canyons, cliffs, and alcoves.

Pinyon pine and juniper are the prominent trees found throughout this area. Ancient cottonwood trees provide mottled shade along waterways and side canyons. Yuccas shoot up stalks of orchid-like flowers, edible to area wildlife. Pops of color in the spring from scarlet gilia draw the eye from far away. The fragrance of cliffrose bushes inspires you to take a deep breath as you enjoy the splendor in the diversity of plants and animals found in this region.

If you hike the lower trail, which connects the three bridges together, you will enter a beautiful riparian area as the trail follows White Canyon Creek. The easternmost bridge is named Sipapu, meaning the "place of emergence" in Hopitutskawa (Hopi), the legacy of the Ancestral Puebloans. They believed that this was the entryway from which their ancestors came into this world. The middle bridge is named Kachina, for symbols found on the bridge, which are commonly used in the decoration of kachina dolls. The final bridge is named Owachomo, which means "rock mound." On top of this bridge, you will see a pile of rock, hence the name.

The water found throughout White Canyon draws many desert birds to the area. Woodhouse's jays, pinyon jays, juniper titmice, ash-throated flycatchers, bushtits, and canyon wrens fill these canyons with birdsong. They rely heavily on the water found in this canyon and the insects that live within the area. On a full moon night in the spring, many of these birds will call all night long. Diurnal animals are often active beneath the light of a full moon, but stay dormant under a new moon.

Wherever you travel throughout the Southwest, you will uncover stories in the landscape—stories of ancient times and ancient peoples, outlaws running from the law, cowboys ranching the meadows, miners dreaming of wealth, farmers growing produce under harsh conditions, and homesteaders dreaming of land of their own. I hope you enjoy uncovering their stories as you seek natural darkness.

31. BAT WATCHING AT OWACHOMO BRIDGE

With sixteen species of bats utilizing the landscape within the monument during migration, the canyon walls, massive cottonwoods, and many rock outcroppings are prime locations for roosting sites. Bats feed around the bridges and above most of the trees within the monument. Depending on the species, the time of feeding varies; some will feed just after sunset, others not until late in the night or early in the morning.

Activity: Bat watching
Adventure rating: 2
Start: Natural Bridges Loop Road, Owachomo Bridge parking area
Distance: 0.54 mile out and back
Elevation loss: 166 feet
Difficulty: Moderate
Hiking time: About 15 minutes
Best seasons: Summer
Timing: 30 minutes before sunset
Fees and permits: $–$$
Contact: Natural Bridges National Monument visitor center, (435) 692-1234, ext. 616
Dog-friendly: No
Trail surface: Dirt and sandstone
Land status: National monument

Nearest town: Blanding
Other trail users: Hikers, photographers
Maps: www.nps.gov/nabr/planyourvisit/maps.htm
Special considerations: The trail has many stairs to hike to get to this bridge.
Other: If you ever come across a bat on the ground, leave it alone, as it is not healthy. Also avoid going all the way to the bottom if there is precipitation happening.
Supplies to take: Drinking water, binoculars, headlamp with extra batteries, and layers of clothing

FINDING THE TRAILHEAD

From Blanding, take US 191 south to the intersection with UT 95. Turn right onto UT 95. Follow UT 95 roughly 30 miles west of Blanding to UT 275. Turn northwest onto UT 275 and drive 4.7 miles to the visitor center. In another 1.7 miles, the road will become a one-way road. Follow Bridge View Drive for another 5 miles to Owachomo Bridge parking area, which will be on your right.
Owachomo Bridge trailhead GPS: N37 35.110' / W110 00.827'

THE ADVENTURE

From the parking area, head down the trail to Owachomo Bridge. It's a relatively short hike with many stairs to navigate. Getting down there in time to watch the sunset is pure magic. Bathed in orange and red colors, everything glows.

This short trail leads you down along the sandstone to a series of stone steps, then twists down and around a bit more sandstone before dropping into the sandy wash created by flash

LOOK UP
Rayleigh scattering happens when most light waves are refracted due to particulates and water vapor in the low atmosphere, letting through only the slower wavelength of orange and red light waves. That's what makes sunsets so pretty.

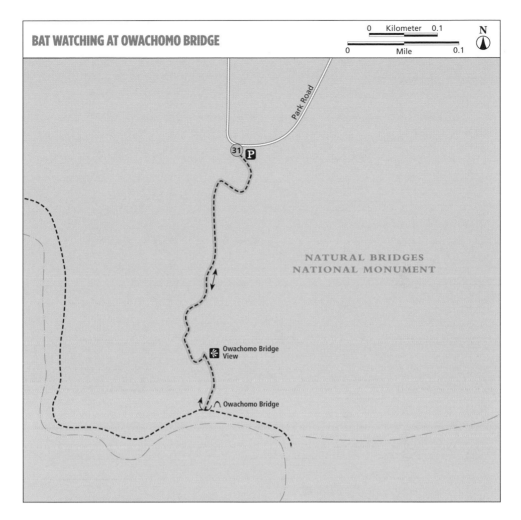

0   Kilometer   0.1

0   Mile   0.1

N

NATURAL BRIDGES
NATIONAL MONUMENT

Owachomo Bridge
View

Owachomo Bridge

flooding. Once in the wash, find a good location to relax while watching the sky above the
bridge. You will begin to see bats flying above
the bridge feeding on insects.

Bats have notoriously been given a bad repu-
tation as evil creatures of the night out to suck
all the blood from your body, or rabid vermin
that cannot see so are sure to get caught in your
hair. The truth is, the bats across the Colorado
Plateau are not vampire bats, but primarily

> Echolocation is using sound
> to bounce off solid objects.
> The echo bounces off the
> object and back to the bat,
> allowing it to determine
> which objects are closer and
> which are farther away, much
> like a submarine using sonar.

obtain subsistence through insects. They also can see as well as you and me with their
eyes. And with echolocation, they can create a picture of where everything is through
soundwaves, making it easy to see every hair on your head.

The night I was there, the bats' flight pattern was pretty erratic, making me think I was likely seeing canyon bats. The small canyon bats seem to fly rather erratically due to their need to scoop up insects in their tail skin before eating them. Their mouth is so small that it is difficult to catch many insects on the fly. The larger myotis bats can maintain a smooth flight pattern, as they are able to catch insects in their mouth without missing a wingbeat. Whichever species you end up seeing, you are sure to be delighted watching them feed around Owachomo Bridge as you wait for the stars to take over the night sky.

LOOK UP
Do you see the bridge of stars across the night sky, the Milky Way? In lore, the Milky Way has been compared to spilt milk, sprinkled flour, and a sparkly river. What do you see when you look at it?

After enjoying the bats, why not stay and enjoy the stars as well? Owachomo Bridge will soon be silhouetted in the night sky, and at the right angle, you can see stars and the bridge.

When you are finished bat watching and stargazing, head back up the trail the way you came.

32. STARGAZING FROM NATURAL BRIDGES CAMPGROUND

The campground found within this monument is one of the absolute best. It's slightly spread out with only thirteen sites total. Each site has a fire pit, tent pad, and metal picnic table; a vault toilet is nearby. Most campsites have ample shade from junipers and pinyon trees with a nice open space to view the night sky. There is no unshielded light nearby, leaving the sky mostly unhindered by artificial light at night.

Activity: Camping
Adventure rating: 1–4 due to nighttime conditions
Start: Natural Bridges National Monument campground
Difficulty: Easy
Best seasons: Any season
Fees and permits: $$; campsites are first-come, first-served, $.
Contact: Natural Bridges National Monument visitor center, (435) 692-1234, ext. 616
Dog-friendly: No
Trail surface: Dirt and sandstone
Land status: National monument

Nearest town: Blanding
Maps: www.nps.gov/nabr/planyourvisit/maps.htm
Special considerations: The nearest services are in Blanding. Be sure to stock up on fuel and any needed supplies for camping before heading out to the monument.
Supplies to take: Drinking water, food, trail map, headlamp with extra batteries, camping and hiking equipment, and anything else you may need for a few days in this beautiful area

FINDING THE TRAILHEAD
From Blanding, take UT 191 south to the intersection with UT 95. Turn right onto UT 95. Follow UT 95 roughly 30 miles west of Blanding to UT 275. Turn northwest onto UT 275 and drive 4.7 miles to the visitor center. In another 0.2 mile, the campground will be on your right.
Natural Bridges campground GPS: N37 12.241' / W109 59.075'

THE ADVENTURE
Enjoying the night sky from your campsite here is delightful. Most of the campsites have a fairly open view of the sky. Grab your red or green light, night sky map, sleeping pad, bag, and pillow and place them where you have the most extensive range of view.

See if you can find the Big Dipper, an asterism of Ursa Major. If you follow the outside of the dipper's cup toward the top of the dipper and beyond, you will see a semi-bright star called Polaris, or the North Star.

If you are facing Polaris, then your left shoulder is facing west, your back south, and your right shoulder east. Polaris is the star at the end of the Little Dipper's handle.

> An asterism is the part of a constellation that is prominent.

Tracing the handle will bring your eyes to the Little Dipper's cup. The stars of the Little Dipper or Ursa Minor have a variety of magnitude, making it more difficult to make out

than the Big Dipper. The two stars that make up the outside of the Little Dipper are a bit brighter. They are called the guardian stars because they revolve around the North Star, watching over it.

As you lie there picking out other constellations, notice that over time the stars seem to shift to the west. This shift is due to the spin of the Earth on its axis. The North Star is the only star that doesn't seem to move.

LOOK UP
The Big Dipper, Draco, and Cassiopeia are all circumpolar constellations, meaning that they circle Polaris (as all other stars do) and are always visible in Utah's night sky.

NIGHT SKY CHALLENGE

Test your knowledge and observation skills with this night sky challenge:

1. Can you follow the curve of the handle of the Big Dipper to the next brightest star, which appears red in color? Which constellation is the red star, Arcturus, a part of?

2. Can you spot the teapot shape that's just above the southern horizon? Which constellation is this a part of?

3. What is the cloudy-looking path that crosses the night sky to the west of the constellation Sagittarius?

Meteors, or falling stars, are primarily made of small bits of dust or ice left behind by comets as they orbit the sun. The Earth moves through the debris left by the comet as it orbits the sun. Some of these bits hit the atmosphere, causing a streak across the night sky. On occasion, that bit of matter may be a larger meteoroid that comes into the atmosphere. Once it is in the atmosphere, it becomes a meteor. If it hits the Earth, it is called a meteorite.

4. Did you see a meteor streak across the sky?

5. Can you find three bright stars that are about the same magnitude almost directly overhead? These stars make up the Summer Triangle. What are their names?

6. Do you see any planets along the ecliptic line—the path the sun and moon take across the sky? Can you name the planets?

7. Can you make out a backward question mark made out of stars? This is the head of Leo. Do you know what animal the constellation Leo is supposed to resemble?

8. Can you find the tiny constellation named Delphinus? What animal does it resemble?

9. Which constellations reside within the arm of the Milky Way?

10. What is your favorite thing that you saw in the night sky tonight?

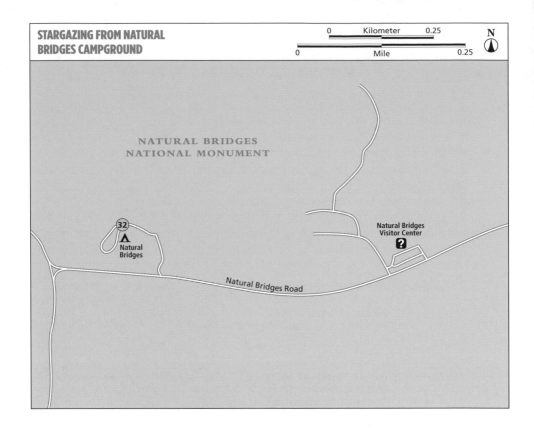

STARGAZING FROM NATURAL BRIDGES CAMPGROUND

Kilometer 0 — 0.25
Mile 0 — 0.25

N

NATURAL BRIDGES
NATIONAL MONUMENT

32
Natural Bridges

Natural Bridges
Visitor Center

Natural Bridges Road

LOOK UP
Now that you have identified Vega, take another look at this blue star. We have found exoplanets forming around Vega. What's an exoplanet? (A planet around another star.) All stars have at least one planet.

Other Opportunities to Enjoy the Night Sky

PARK RANGER–LED EVENTS

During summer, the park offers star parties. These evening events highlight the night sky found within the park and offer the opportunity to look through a telescope at deep space objects such as nebulae, galaxies, star clusters, and more. For more information on the timing of these events, visit www.nps.gov/nabr/planyourvisit/calendar.htm.

GRAND COUNTY

Location: 125 E. Center St., Moab, UT 84532
Dark Sky designation: In process
Contact: www.discovermoab.com

Land status: County
Maps: www.discovermoab.com/maps-and-location-info/

DUE TO THE VAST MAJORITY OF LAND WITHIN GRAND COUNTY being public land, the area is a recreationalist's mecca. With world-class mountain biking, 4x4 off-roading, rock climbing, canyoneering, whitewater rafting, ultra-running, flatwater kayaking, stand-up paddleboarding, and some of the most incredible night skies found in the United States, it's difficult to resist the allure of this area.

Grand County has long been home to Puebloan people of the past and present. Scenes created on rock faces are scattered throughout the county. Many explorers came to rely

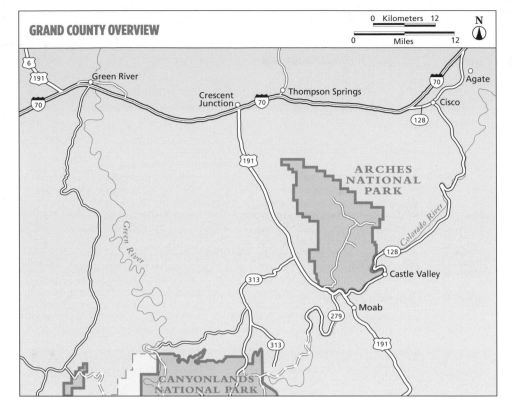

on Ute and Paiute guides for route finding through the rugged desert landscape. Home-steaders, ranchers, and farmers settled much of the land, leaving remnant orchards scattered across the verdant valleys.

During the uranium boom in the United States, this area was filled with active mines extracting the precious element from the earth. From the early 1950s until the 1970s, several miners in the area made millions of dollars off uranium ore—no one more than Charlie Steen, who found his first mining site with a Geiger counter.

With the salt-laden Paradox Formation holding ancient salts from the inland seas that used to cover much of southeastern Utah, potash mining still continues today. This cash crop fertilizer is a staple of the modern farmer's soil amendments. Potash is also used for salt licks for livestock and as road salt.

Bighorn sheep scramble across rocky slopes, blending into the surroundings when motionless. Peregrine falcons screech as they dive, talons clasped in a harrowing act of courtship. A kit fox trots along through the sagebrush with a desert cottontail held in its jaw. A black-chinned hummingbird sips nectar from the trumpet-shaped flowers of the claret cup cactus. Life is abundant in this seemingly deserted landscape. At night, the secret world comes alive with wildlife foraging, mating, surviving, and resting beneath a blanket of stars.

There is something special about being surrounded by the red sandstone under the typical blue sky. The contrasting colors make every view seem like a masterpiece. Lying on your back against the sandstone, soaking in the heat like a lizard, places you into a deep relaxation. And with so much public land, there will always be new places to explore every time you visit.

33. FLATWATER PADDLE THROUGH LABYRINTH CANYON

Following in John Wesley Powell's paddle strokes is a memorable adventure. A trip through Labyrinth Canyon is a wonderful way to get into a more remote landscape fast. This section of the Green River is full of history. Plan some time to explore the side canyons, historic inscriptions, and mining sites. Relax and take in the feeling of a slower pace of life. Embrace the silence of the desert and listen for the life that lives there. Powell would have looked up at the same stars you will see at night, pondering similar questions to what you may have about the cosmos.

Activity: Flatwater paddle
Adventure rating: 3
Start: Green River State Park
Distance: 68.31 miles one way
Elevation loss: 96 feet
Difficulty: Moderate
Paddle time: 4 days and 3 nights
Best seasons: Late spring, summer, and early fall
Timing: Any time
Fees and permits: $
River contacts: BLM Moab field office, (435) 259-2100
Dog-friendly: No
Water surface: Flatwater
Land status: Bureau of Land Management
Nearest town: Green River
Other river users: None

Maps: www.blm-egis.maps.arcgis.com/apps/webappviewer/index.html?id=6f0da4c7931440a8a80bfe20eddd7550
Special considerations: You will need to leave a shuttle vehicle at the Mineral Bottom boat ramp.
Other: Make sure you have everything required on the BLM permit.
Supplies to take: Boat, paddle, life jacket, dry bags for all gear, tent, sleeping bag and pad, pot, stove, utensils, backpacking food, water, water filter, snacks, electrolytes, first-aid kit, pepper spray, layers of clothing, boating sandals, waterproof matches, knife, map, compass, hiking shoes, and any personal items

FINDING THE PUT-IN/TAKEOUT
Green River boat ramp GPS: N38 59.320' / W110 09.021'

Green River State Park in Green River Utah put-in
Green River Boulevard off Main Street in Green River leads to Green River State Park. Once through the entrance gate, follow the road to the boat ramp.

Mineral Bottom takeout
Head north on US 191 from Moab. In 11.0 miles, turn left onto UT 313. Follow UT 313 for 12.3 miles and turn right onto BLM 129/Mineral Canyon Road. Follow Mineral Canyon Road for 15.5 miles. At the end, the road drops down narrow switchbacks to river level. Once down, stay right and follow Mineral Canyon Road to the boat ramp.

Desert varnish is a substance formed on cliffsides when cyanobacteria create a sticky surface for manganese and iron along with sand grains to collect on, looking like black streaks down the canyon walls.

THE ADVENTURE

From Green River State Park's boat ramp, load up your boat with all your camping and river gear. The first 4 miles will give you a good idea of how well you've packed your boat. Does any section of the boat look too low in the water? If so, you may have to shift your gear bags around a bit. It's best to figure this out right away.

About 4 miles into the journey, you will pass an area with minerals coating the rock on river left. This is Crystal Geyser, an abandoned test well that still has an occasional release of water in geyser form. Right after the geyser area, you will come to a riffle called the Auger; stay to the side in this section.

The first section of this trip is through a wide-open landscape. You can still see the tenacious green of area agriculture along the riverbanks. Ten miles in you will begin to see the gray and green Morrison Formation. This area is known to contain dinosaur tracks, though none have been found along the river's edge.

> **LOOK UP**
>
> I often puzzle at all the possibilities for life that exist in our solar system. If Saturn and Jupiter are visible in the night sky, ponder the fact that both have an icy moon where life is possible—Saturn's moon Enceladus and Jupiter's moon Europa. Both of these icy moons have liquid water oceans that could be teeming with life.

At mile 18.5, Dellenbaugh Butte comes into view, a high butte on river left. This formation was named by John Wesley Powell for the youngest member of his expedition, seventeen-year-old Frederick Dellenbaugh.

At mile 23, the San Rafael River pours into the Green from river right. If there has been recent rain or snowmelt, the extra water may cause some riffles in this area. Most of the summer, though, the transition is a gentle one. From this point, the canyon walls begin to rise, and desert varnish starts to appear on the Navajo Sandstone on river left.

The next 5 miles offer several options for camping. Finding a site with a nice sandy beach is best. These beaches are normally bug-free, meaning a better opportunity to sleep out under the stars.

At mile 30, on river right, you will come to Trin-Alcove, a three-canyon system. This is a great spot to stop and stretch your legs. In the spring you can paddle upcanyon for quite a ways.

The rest of the trip offers loads of exploration, so take your time.

Over the next few miles, just relax and take in the remoteness of the area. On river right, the next big canyon is Bull Hollow, a short 1-mile canyon that begs to be explored. Three miles past that, Tenmile Canyon is on river

LOOK UP
See if you can spot the star Vega in the night sky. The Kepler space telescope has been searching the stars around this area for exoplanets in the Goldilocks Zone. It discovered that every star has at least one planet.

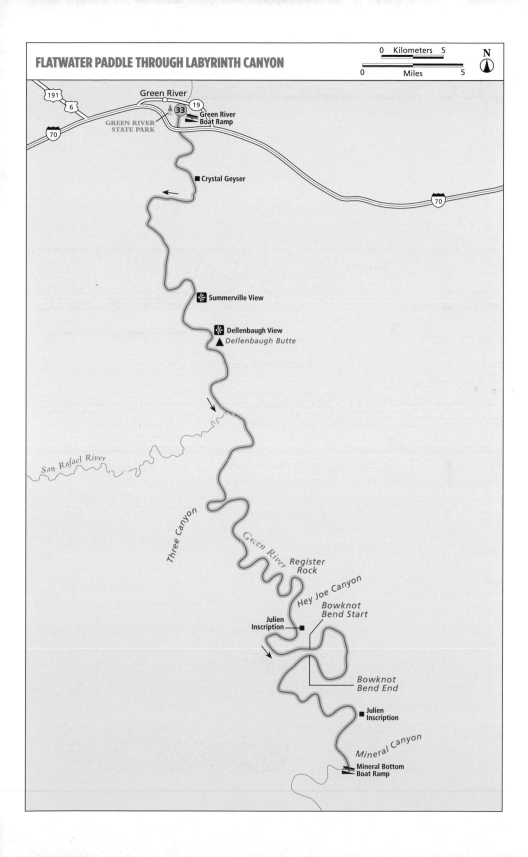

FLATWATER PADDLE THROUGH LABYRINTH CANYON

0   Kilometers   5
0   Miles   5

N

191
6
70

Green River

33   19
Green River
Boat Ramp

GREEN RIVER
STATE PARK

70

■ Crystal Geyser

Summerville View

Dellenbaugh View
▲ Dellenbaugh Butte

San Rafael River

Three Canyon

Green River

Register
Rock

Hey Joe Canyon

Bowknot
Bend Start

Julien
Inscription ■

Bowknot
Bend End

■ Julien
Inscription

Mineral Canyon

Mineral Bottom
Boat Ramp

left. You could easily spend a half day exploring this side canyon. This is a great spot to camp for the night.

At 42.9 miles, on river left, is Register Rock. This cliff face has historically been used by those coming down the river to record their passing. You will see many dates from the late 1800s to early 1900s. There are even a few pieces of artwork on the wall. This practice is not encouraged today; please just observe the markings that are there without adding your own.

Another 2 miles downriver, on river left, is Hey Joe Canyon. This canyon had an active uranium mine for many years. Much of the mining camp and equipment can still be found in this location.

At mile 50.4, Bowknot Bend begins. This 7-mile bend in the river takes a while to travel around. A quick hike from river right will take you up to the ridgeline, where you can see both sides of the river in a single view.

At mile 60 you will come to Horseshoe Canyon on river right. This is a wonderful spot to camp and explore for the rest of the day.

> This is an abandoned meander of the Green River. The river used to flow around the butte you can see at the end of Horseshoe Canyon but has since changed course to abandon the route. You can follow the old riverbed around for about 3 miles on foot.

About 4.5 miles from here, on river left, is Hell Roaring Canyon. This is a wonderful chance to stop and explore an inscription left by Denis Julien, a fur trapper who ran many of the river routes in the area. You will find the inscription on the Hell Roaring Canyon wall, facing north about 300 feet from the Green River.

Another 2 miles downriver is the Mineral Bottom boat ramp, your takeout. Now the work of derigging and packing up your vehicle begins. Don't forget, you'll need to pick up your other vehicle from Green River State Park.

MILES AND DIRECTIONS

0.0   Start at the Green River State Park boat ramp.

18.42   Dellenbaugh Butte view.

23.33   The San Rafael River enters the Green River on river right.

42.93   Register Rock; make a quick stop to see the historic names on the cliff wall.

50.41   Bowknot Bend ridge hike and the start of Bowknot Bend.

57.66   End of the Bowknot Bend.

68.31   Arrive at the Mineral Bottom boat ramp.

34. ASTROPHOTOGRAPHY FROM MARLBORO POINT

Made famous by the iconic Marlboro Man, a Western cowboy riding his horse through the desert landscape to this jaw-dropping vista, Marlboro Point provides the perfect foreground for an incredible astrophotography session. Big Mesa comes to an abrupt end, with sheer cliffs dropping over 400 feet to Shafer Canyon below. Looking outward from the cliff edge, you can see Crow's Head Spire and Bird's Eye Butte jutting out from the cliff.

Activity: 4x4 drive for astrophotography
Adventure rating: 3
Start: US 191 northwest of Moab
Distance: 6.74 miles out and back
Elevation gain: 26 feet
Difficulty: Moderate
Trip time: About 1 hour
Best seasons: Any season if the roads are dry
Timing: Any time of the night
Fees and permits: Free
Trail contacts: BLM Moab field office, (435) 259-2100
Dog-friendly: Yes; clean up and pack out pet (and human) waste.
Trail surface: Dirt, sand, and rock
Land status: Bureau of Land Management
Nearest town: Moab
Other trail users: Mountain bikers, OHVs, motorcycles, hikers

Maps: www.blm-egis.maps.arcgis.com/apps/webappviewer/index.html?id=6f0da4c7931440a8a80bfe20eddd7550
Special considerations: If the roads are wet, do not attempt this drive to avoid damaging the roads or getting stuck in this remote area.
Other: Be mindful of your surroundings. This landscape is rugged, and a misstep can result in injury. There are a few deep cracks in the sandstone, so use a headlamp to access your photography spot. Be mindful of your steps.
Supplies to take: Drinking water, salty snacks, camera, lenses, headlamp with extra batteries, high-clearance 4x4 with emergency equipment in case it breaks down, and gear to pack out if needed

FINDING THE TRAILHEAD

From Moab, follow US 191 northwest toward Canyonlands National Park. After passing Arches National Park, the road climbs to a plateau. Start watching for a large brown sign that indicates the turn for Canyonlands National Park and Dead Horse Point State Park. Turn left just past the Moab Giants dinosaur museum onto UT 313. Follow UT 313 toward Dead Horse Point State Park. At the top of the mesa, make a left-hand turn to stay on UT 313 toward the state park. Just after passing Long Canyon Road, look for an oil well road on the next rise. This is the start of the 4x4 adventure.
Marlboro Point route start GPS: N38 29.704' / W109 46.174'

THE ADVENTURE

Marlboro Point gives photographers a 360-degree view of the night sky with a low horizon line on all sides. During the summer months of August and September, the Milky Way stretches directly overhead, with the galactic center being straight south. South of

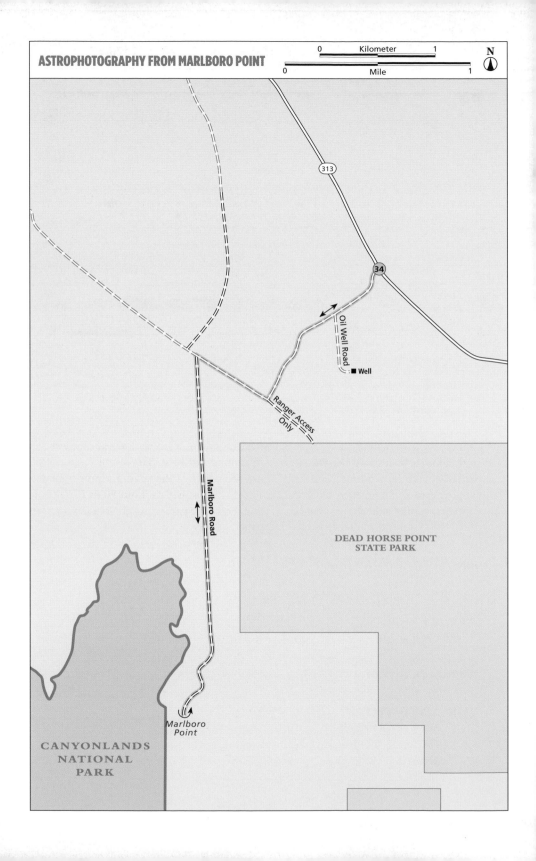

0 Kilometer 1

0 Mile 1

N

313

34

Oil Well Road

■ Well

Ranger Access
Only

Marlboro Road

DEAD HORSE POINT
STATE PARK

Marlboro
Point

CANYONLANDS
NATIONAL
PARK

Marlboro Point, there is nothing but public lands for approximately 100 miles, until the Diné Bikéyah (Navajo) reservation near the Arizona border.

From UT 313, follow the oil well road until it begins to curve toward the well. Directly west, a 4-wheel-drive road will appear. Take that road as it curves around the well site, and continue southward before intersecting another dirt road. Turn right (west) at the junction with this road. Follow this road until you see an earthen dam on your right and another dirt road branching off to the left (south); this is the Marlboro Point Road. Follow this rough 4-wheel-drive road to the end. From the parking area it is a few steps to the edge of the cliff to set up for your astrophotography shoot.

Camping is not allowed on Marlboro Point. The nearest campsites are at Dead Horse Point State Park or Cowboy Camp on BLM land.

MILES AND DIRECTIONS

0.0 Start at the UT 313 and oil well road junction.

0.35 Junction with the oil well road and a 4x4 road; stay right and follow the 4x4 road.

0.97 Junction with a 4x4 road; turn right.

1.41 Junction with 4x4 road and Marlboro Point Road; turn left and continue south until you reach Marlboro Point.

3.37 Reach Marlboro Point. Return the way you came.

6.74 Arrive back at UT 313.

35. ASTROPHOTOGRAPHY AT WARNER LAKE

High in the La Sal Mountains, nestled into the hillside, is Warner Lake. Haystack Mountain reflecting off the surface of this small mountain lake presents gorgeous nighttime photos. On a new moon night, if there is no breeze, you can even get starlight reflecting on the surface of the lake, creating incredible nightscapes. The cooler summer temperatures also make this a favorite camping spot among locals.

Activity: Astrophotography
Adventure rating: 1
Start: Warner Lake Campground
Distance: 0.13 mile out and back
Difficulty: Easy
Time: 1–6 hours
Best seasons: Late spring, summer, and early fall
Timing: Any time of the night
Fees and permits: $
Contact: Moab field office, (435) 259-7155
Dog-friendly: Yes; clean up and pack out pet waste.
Trail surface: Dirt
Land status: National forest

Nearest town: Moab
Other trail users: Mountain bikers, hikers, anglers, photographers
Maps: www.fs.usda.gov/recarea/mantilasal/recreation/camping-cabins/recarea/?recid=73218&actid=29
Special considerations: If the roads have snow on them, the gate will be closed far below.
Other: Be mindful of your surroundings.
Supplies to take: Drinking water, salty snacks, camera, extra camera battery, tripod, headlamp with extra batteries

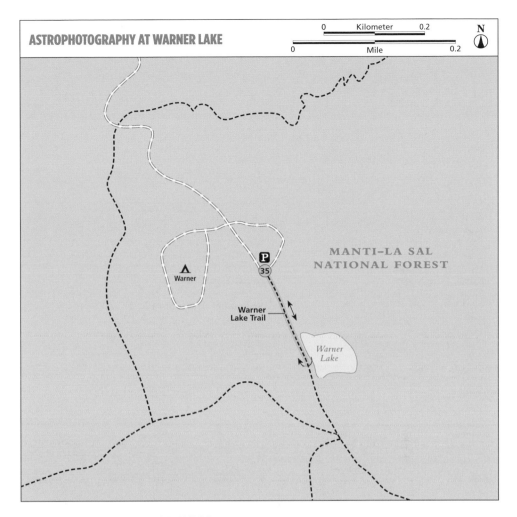

FINDING THE TRAILHEAD

From Moab, head south along US 191. Turn left when you see the sign indicating La Sal Loop Road. You will pass a large construction company before coming to the road. Turn right and follow this road up and into the La Sal Mountains for 5.37 miles until the turn for Warner Lake Campground. Turn right and head up the dirt road. The road climbs for several miles before arriving at the Warner Lake Campground. Make sure to park in the day-use lot and pay the fee in the box before heading out to the lake.

Warner Lake trailhead GPS: N38 31.172' / W109 16.541'

THE ADVENTURE

Once at the day-use parking area, load up your gear and head out on the trail. You will cross an open meadow toward the tree line of aspen trees ahead. Just before reaching these trees, you will come to Warner Lake. Make sure to find a firm area away from the inlet and outlet streams to set up for the night.

MOAB

Location: 217 E. Center St., Moab, UT 84532
Dark Sky designation: In process
Contact: City of Moab, www.discovermoab.com

Land status: Municipal
Maps: www.discovermoab.com/maps-and-location-info/

A COMMUNITY OF ABOUT 5,300 PEOPLE, Moab is considered an outdoor recreation mecca. The red rock adventures found in this landscape bring world-class athletes to test their skills against one of the most challenging landscapes of the Colorado Plateau.

Moab also just happens to be next to two the most popular national parks in the southwestern United States: Arches and Canyonlands National Parks. People from all over the world flock to see the natural wonders in these two parks. Arches National Park has more than 2,000 natural arches to see and explore. Canyonlands National Park has hoodoos, spires, deep canyons, and the Colorado and Green Rivers to explore.

The rivers near Moab offer visitors the opportunity to enjoy single-day and multiday tours of flatwater or whitewater on the Green and Colorado Rivers. These trips will transport you through landscapes steeped in history, archaeology, natural history, and a layer cake of geological time spanning hundreds of millions of years ago to the present.

At night, much of the greater Moab area hosts one of the darkest night skies found in the United States. Just 20 minutes outside the town, the night sky comes alive with planets, stars, the moon, satellites, the ISS, and the occasional meteor.

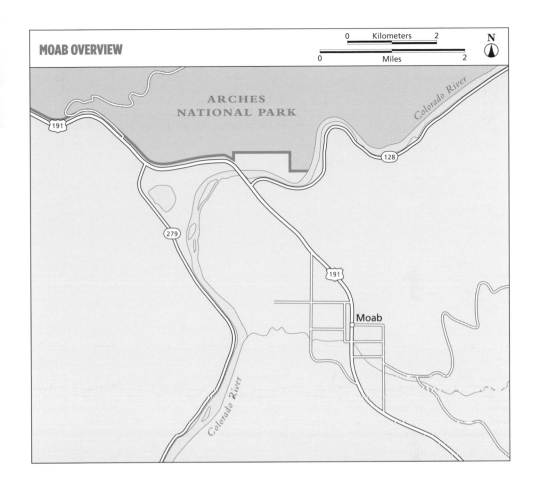

MOAB OVERVIEW

ARCHES
NATIONAL PARK

Colorado River

191

128

279

191

Moab

Colorado River

Kilometers

Miles

N

The community is a green community, with most of its electricity coming from solar farms nearby. It also strives to be a certified sustainable community. The commitment to reducing its global footprint is commendable. Protection of the natural darkness around the city and county has also been initiated, a feat that failed several times before—proof that tenacity is required to bring about lasting change.

LOOK UP
Meteors are typically just fine pieces of dust and ice that burn up when they hit the atmosphere. The larger "fireballs" are usually only the size of a golf ball.

Whether you come to Moab to mountain bike the Slickrock Trail or run the rapids of Cataract Canyon, the place is sure to leave you with a desire to return over and over again. Don't forget to spend some of your time out underneath the starry night sky. Seeing the Milky Way stretch across a dark sky is something everyone should experience.

36. **FULL MOON HIKE TO CORONA ARCH**

Corona Arch is undoubtedly one of the most beautiful arches in the greater Moab area. Looking much like saltwater taffy that has been stretched away from the vertical cliff, the arch spans 140 feet across and stands 105 feet high. Just next door to Corona Arch is the beautiful Bowtie Arch, created by an ephemeral pool wearing through the rock layer. A small opening in the roof of the cliff above a striped desert seep with maidenhair ferns growing out of it, Corona Arch is a stunner to photograph. In the spring, you may find monkeyflower growing below the seep.

Activity: Full moon hike
Adventure rating: 4
Start: Corona Arch trailhead
Distance: 2.12 miles out and back
Elevation gain: 378 feet
Difficulty: Moderate
Hiking time: About 2 hours
Best seasons: Spring, summer, and fall
Timing: Be at the trailhead ready to roll by sunset.
Dog-friendly: No, due to exposure and pitch
Trail surface: Dirt and rock
Fees and permits: Free
Contact: BLM Moab field office, (435) 259-2100
Land status: Bureau of Land Management

Nearest town: Moab
Other trail users: Hikers only
Maps: www.blm.gov/visit/corona-arch-trail
Special considerations: The end of the trail has several sections with a steep pitch and exposure to cliffs. If you are afraid of heights, hike the trail during the day to see if you will be okay at night.
Other: Be mindful of your surroundings. This landscape is rugged, and a misstep can result in injury.
Supplies to take: Drinking water, salty snacks, trail map, camera with extra battery, tripod, and headlamp with extra batteries

FINDING THE TRAILHEAD
From Moab, head north along UT 191. After crossing the Colorado River Bridge, watch for the turn onto UT 279/Potash Road. Turn left onto UT 279 and follow the road until you reach the Corona Arch trailhead above and across from Gold Bar Campground.
Corona Arch trailhead GPS: N38 34.801' / W109 37.244'

THE ADVENTURE
Start this hike just before sunset. This will give you enough time to hike in during the daylight and see the route clearly before darkness sets in.

The trail begins with a quick hike along a rocky slope up to the level of a set of railroad tracks. After crossing the tracks, the trail heads into a small canyon and widens for a bit. At the end of the canyon, you will climb another rocky section through a sandstone wash. Once topping out of this section, the vista opens up all around you. Turn around for a gorgeous view of the Colorado River below before continuing up the trail.

BOWTIE ARCH

FULL MOON HIKE TO CORONA ARCH

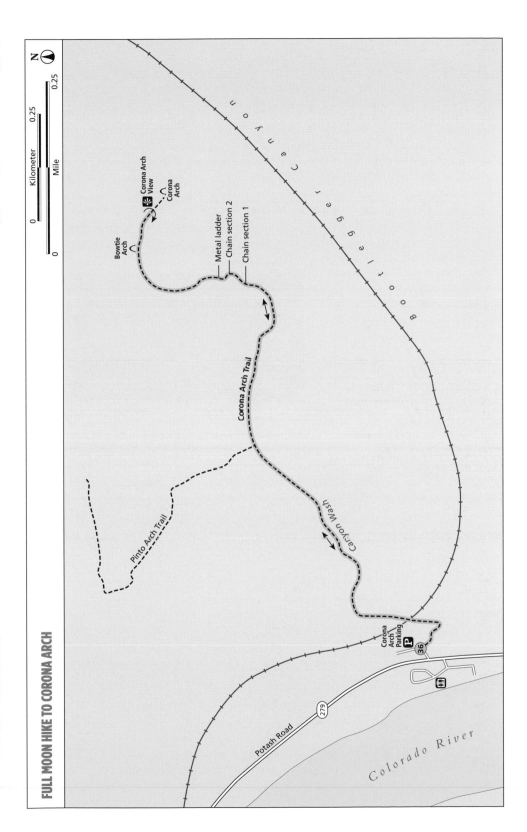

The railroad tracks lead to the potash plant found at the end of the paved road. This plant produces 1.1 million tons of potash per year, a salt compound that is used as a fertilizer for most cash crops, such as corn.

Once you cross another vast expanse of sandstone, you will come around the corner to a section of chains. The pitch of this section is a bit strong, so chains have been placed to ensure you do not slip and fall. A short stint brings you to the next set of chains, which are on a nearly vertical slope; steps have been carved into the sandstone to assist your footing while holding onto the chains to climb up this section. The trail continues to a small metal ladder that tops out at another steep climb up the sandstone. This climb does not have chains, so please be mindful of your footing. Once up this short, steep pitch, the trail levels out at the level of the arch. Follow the natural form of the sandstone here as it curves around to the arch.

Enjoy watching the last glow of sunlight on the arch before the moonlight takes over. As night falls throughout the canyon, it is amazing how much you can see by the light of the full moon. Seek out your own shadow. It's a thrill to return to childhood for a brief moment while creating shadow animals.

LOOK UP
Luna reflects the light of our sun, which makes it seem as if it is glowing. This same reflected sunlight is what makes the planets glimmer in the night sky. Sunlight is reflected off their atmosphere or surface, making them shine bright.

When you are ready, head back the way you came. Use extra caution while returning through the first 0.25 mile of technical moves. Once back to the car, pause and take in the night sky once more. Remember your origins are in the night sky. You are made up of the elements created in the violent death of massive stars. You are the universe manifesting itself in flesh and blood.

MILES AND DIRECTIONS

0.0 Start at the Corona Arch trailhead.

0.1 Railroad track crossing.

0.31 Scramble up the dry canyon wash.

0.77 First section of chains.

0.8 Second section of chains.

0.83 Climb a metal ladder.

1.0 Bowtie Arch.

1.06 Reach the Corona Arch view; return the way you came.

2.12 Arrive back at the Corona Arch trailhead.

37. **FLATWATER PADDLE FROM BIG BEND TO COLORADO RIVER BRIDGE**

Floating the flatwater sections of the Colorado River at night is a definite adventure to experience. Sightings of American beavers are common along the river. You can often see their burrows in the bank behind the roots of trees. The slap of their tail on the water's surface will definitely wake you up.

Activity: Night flatwater paddle
Adventure rating: 3
Start: Boat ramp at Big Bend Campground
Distance: 7.38 miles one way
Difficulty: Easy
Paddling time: About 3 hours
Best seasons: Late spring and summer
Timing: A few days before the full moon to the full moon; just after sunset
Fees and permits: Free
Contact: BLM Moab field office
Dog-friendly: Yes, if your dog is an experienced boater
Water surface: Flatwater
Land status: Bureau of Land Management
Nearest town: Moab

Other river users: Jet boats, tour boats, SUPs
Maps: www.southwestpaddler.com/docs/coloradout3.html
Special considerations: Take the time to scout the route during the day. The river can change overnight if boulders fall into the water or trees are swept into the river by flash floods. You will need to leave a shuttle vehicle at the Colorado River Bridge before heading to the boat ramp.
Other: Be mindful of your surroundings at all times. Jet boats and tour boats come through this section of river often. Make sure to turn your headlamp on if you hear a boat motor to increase visibility.
Supplies to take: Drinking water, salty snacks, headlamp with extra batteries, life vest, boat, and shuttle vehicle

FINDING THE PUT-IN

From Moab, head north until you reach UT 128. Turn right onto UT 128 and follow it to Big Bend Campground. Turn left once into the campground. Turn left again and follow the campground road to the small boat ramp on the right.
Big Bend boat ramp GPS: N38 38.935' / W109 28.763'

THE ADVENTURE

I suggest launching just after sunset. This will give you a bit of light to make it through the first few riffles if the water is low. (You may need to see the rocks that cause them.) Right after launching from the boat ramp, you will come to a riffle (too small to be categorized as a rapid) followed by two other much smaller riffles. After that, the water becomes very still, requiring a little paddling to keep moving forward.

For the next 4 miles, the route is straight, providing a long view down the river. This is a great time to watch for beavers swimming in the moonlight. If you happen to startle them, you'll hear a loud slap on the water as an alert to all the other beavers that something dangerous is coming their way.

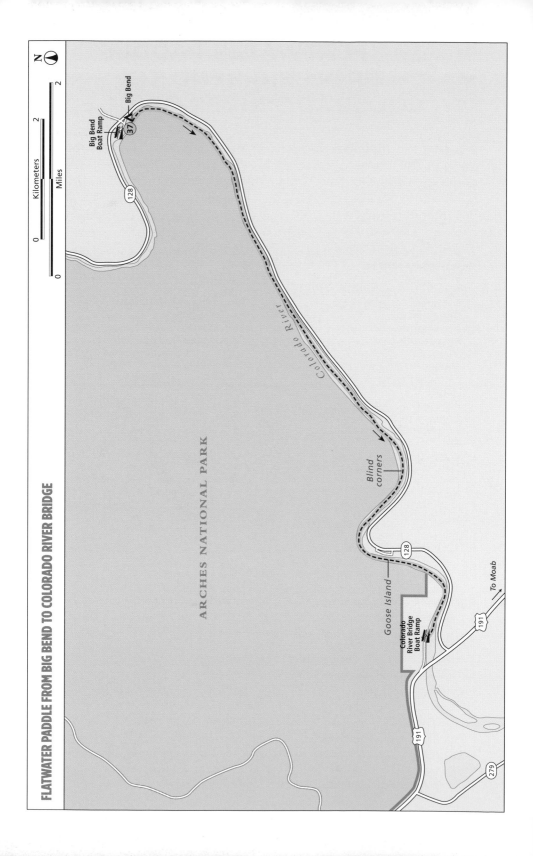

FLATWATER PADDLE FROM BIG BEND TO COLORADO RIVER BRIDGE

N

Kilometers
0   2

Miles
0   2

Big Bend

Big Bend
Boat Ramp

37

128

Colorado River

ARCHES NATIONAL PARK

Blind
corners

Goose Island

128

Colorado
River Bridge
Boat Ramp

To Moab

191

191

279

The last glow of orange from the cliffs reflects in the water before you. Soon after, your eyes will begin to transition into "night mode." For about 15 minutes, it will be difficult to see. Floating until they adjust is a grand idea.

Then the show really begins—the moonlight playing off the water. As a person obsessed with the reflection of light and the patterns it creates, I find it a thrilling experience to be floating down the river on a white ribbon of shifting light coming from Luna.

LOOK UP
The mares of the moon are not actually smooth lake bottoms, but rather basalt fields from when the moon was volcanically active. The basalt boulders were a bit of a problem for Neil Armstrong when trying to land the lunar lander on the moon.

The last 2 miles of the trip have a few bends in the river. There are several tours that come up the river in the evening, so it is a good idea to stay close to the bank through this section. If you hear a motor, turn on your headlamp so they can see where you are and alert them to your presence.

You'll know without a doubt when you've arrived at the boat ramp, as you'll be able to see the art pieces on the pedestrian bridge ahead, which are lit up by a small solar light. It's time to pull up to the ramp and exit the boat.

MILES AND DIRECTIONS

0.0 Start at the Big Bend boat ramp.

4.3 The blind corners begin.

6.16 Goose Island Campground.

7.38 Arrive at the Colorado River Bridge boat ramp, the end of the adventure.

The American beaver was almost trapped out of existence when the demand for their waterproof pelt was high. Colorado River beavers often make burrows in the banks of the river. They also make channels vertical to the river to bring large trees back to their dam often along the bank.

DEAD HORSE POINT STATE PARK

Location: SR 313, Moab, UT 84532
Dark Sky designation: 2016
Contact: Dead Horse Point State
Park visitor center, (435) 259-2614

Land status: State park
Maps: https://stateparks.utah.gov/
parks/dead-horse/map/

RISING 2,000 FEET ABOVE THE COLORADO RIVER, Dead Horse Point State
Park has long captured the attention of people visiting the Moab area. Walking out to
the Point, you are walking on the same surface that dinosaurs once crossed. The view
from the Point itself looks out over a gooseneck bend in the Colorado River. The cliffside reveals massive ancient sand dunes cemented into stone. Below the cliffs you'll find
an ancient swamp environment rich in uranium, petrified wood, and unoxidized iron.
Below that, ancient mudflats stretch horizontal through the landscape. An ancient river-
way with its massive deltas make up the next layer down, followed by an ancient seabed
filled with crinoid and shellfish fossils at river level.

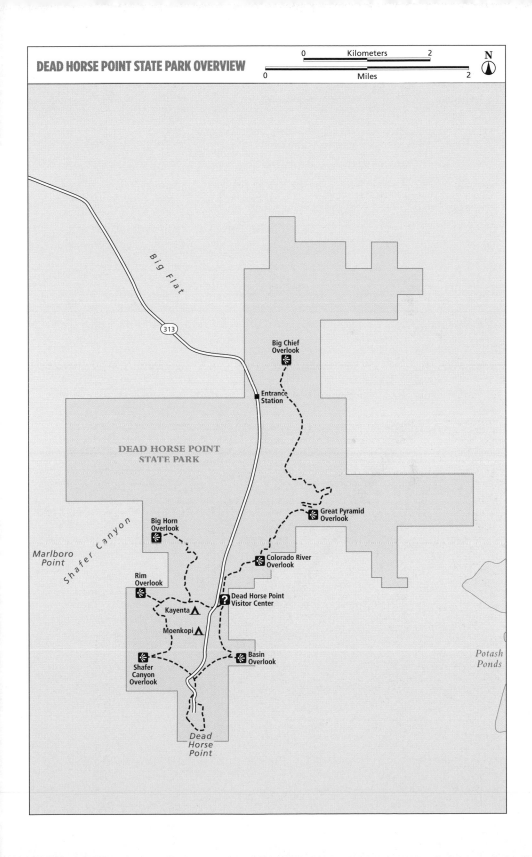

Archaic people were known to wander the cliffs within this park while hunting and foraging in the area. Evidence of this has been found in the tools and other artifacts left behind. Ancestral Puebloans also used the area to hunt bighorn sheep and deer and forage for plants. Today, foraging in these ancestral ways continues for the Hopitutskwa (Hopi) people.

Historically, this area was used for ranging livestock, much as the landscape outside the park still is used. Evidence of this can be seen by the large stretches of open meadow where once there was a pinyon-juniper forest. Ranchers use to drag chains through areas on the mesa to create higher-altitude meadows for livestock.

Today this area is home to bighorn sheep, mule deer, bobcats, coyotes, kit foxes, ringtails, lizards, birds, and many smaller mammals. Peregrine falcons and golden eagles nest within the cliffs of the park. Below, in Shafer Canyon, on rare occasions you might hear two bighorn rams butting heads, the sound reverberating like a shotgun firing into the air.

People from all over the world come to Dead Horse Point each year to see the iconic view filmed in *Thelma and Louise*, *Mission Impossible III*, *The Lone Ranger*, and more Hollywood films. A small handful will stay to truly experience all this park has to offer. The night sky is incredible within the park, something I had everything to do with while working as a park ranger here. Whether you enjoy mountain biking, hiking, camping, scenic driving, or glamping, this small park has plenty to offer.

38. NIGHT HIKE TO RIM OVERLOOK

If you want to see wildlife in the desert, it is best to hike in the early evening or early morning. Most desert animals are active during the twilight hours in the desert. Your best chance of seeing them is during the time between day and night.

Looking down into Shafer Canyon from the Rim Overlook over a 400-foot cliff reminds you quickly that you are alive. Looking south, you can see Dark Horse Spire and just past that the Colorado River. To the west and south, you are looking at nothing but public lands for many miles, leaving you with a Bortle Class 2 sky, a sky slightly touched with light pollution, a sky one step away from being untouched by artificial light at night.

Activity: Night hike
Adventure rating: 2
Start: West Rim trailhead
Distance: 1.86 miles out and back
Elevation gain: 41 feet
Difficulty: Moderate
Hiking time: About 1.5 hours
Best seasons: Spring, summer, and fall
Timing: Be at the trailhead ready to roll by sunset.
Dog-friendly: Yes, must be on 6-foot leash and under control
Fees and permits: $$
Contact: Dead Horse Point State Park visitor center, (435) 259-2614
Land status: State park

Nearest town: Moab
Other trail users: None
Maps: https://stateparks.utah.gov/parks/dead-horse/map/
Special considerations: The park closes at 10 p.m. for day-use visitation. During the summer months, you will need to camp to complete this adventure.
Other: Be mindful of your surroundings. This landscape is rugged, and a misstep can result in injury.
Supplies to take: Drinking water, salty snacks, headlamp with extra batteries, and night sky map

FINDING THE TRAILHEAD

From Moab follow US 191 north to the junction with UT 313. Turn left and follow UT 313 to the top of the mesa. As you reach the top, don't miss the left turn to stay on UT 313. Follow UT 313 to the Dead Horse Point visitor center to park. The trailhead is behind the visitor center on the east side of the building.
West Rim trailhead GPS: N38 29.260' / W109 44.145'

THE ADVENTURE

This adventure begins on the east side of the visitor center. There you will find the trailhead for the West Rim Trail. Head up the trail while keeping an eye above the trees. You will most likely see canyon bats flying over the trees scooping up insects along the way. Once you cross UT 313, you will be skirting the Kayenta Campground.

> Keep your eyes open for eyeshine from an animal in your headlamp beam and your ears open for sounds of wildlife.

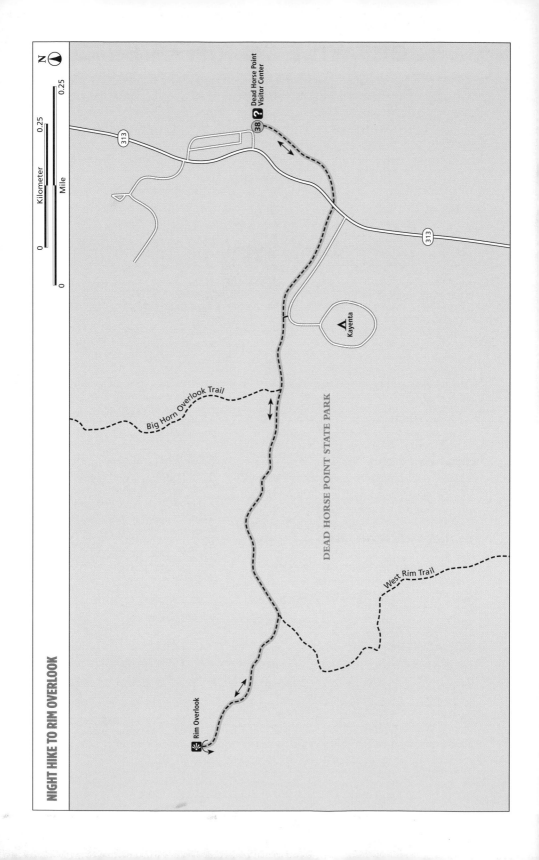

NIGHT HIKE TO RIM OVERLOOK

Once past the campground, you will come to a junction with the Bighorn Overlook Trail; stay left and continue on the West Rim Trail. You will cross some sandstone, drop down a few steps, and come to another sandstone flat. There you will find the junction with the Rim Overlook Trail. Turn right onto this trail and follow it to the canyon rim.

> On the rim, find a spot to lie down and stargaze. The more I learn about our universe, the more I'm drawn to stargaze. The mysteries that are still present give you pause to ponder and theorize your ideas.

MILES AND DIRECTIONS

0.0 Start at the Dead Horse Point visitor center. Hike just a little east to pick up the West Rim Trail.

0.15 Cross UT 313.

0.31 Pass the connector trail to Kayenta Campground.

0.39 Junction with Bighorn Overlook Trail; stay left on the West Rim Trail.

0.71 Junction with Rim Trail; turn right and hike west along this trail.

0.93 Reach the Rim Overlook; return the way you came.

1.86 Arrive back at the visitor center.

39. SCORPION HUNT ON DEAD HORSE POINT

Adapting to the harsh realities of living in the desert, scorpions are one of the most well-adapted desert dwellers in the Moab area. They can go without food for months without dying. Their body shifts into a torpor, a temporary lower metabolic state, until conditions improve. Scorpions can be found in rock outcroppings, on sun-warmed walls, beneath rocks and shrubs, or walking out in the open. Using a black-light highlights the scorpion, as their exoskeleton fluoresces. They will glow a nice bright green color. If you keep your distance, you may get to watch them for quite a while. Remember that this is their home and you are the visitor; give them space to behave naturally.

Activity: Scorpion hunt
Adventure rating: 1
Start: Dead Horse Point picnic area
Distance: None
Difficulty: Easy
Trip time: About 30 minutes
Best seasons: Late spring, summer, and early fall
Timing: About 1 hour after sunset
Fees and permits: $$
Trail contacts: Dead Horse Point State Park visitor center, (435) 259-2614
Dog-friendly: No
Land status: State park
Nearest town: Moab
Other area users: Picnickers, hikers

Maps: https://stateparks.utah.gov/parks/dead-horse/map/
Special considerations: The park closes at 10 p.m. for day-use visitation. During the summer months, you will need to camp to complete this adventure.
Other: Scorpions are wild animals and protected within the park. Remember not to touch them or harass them in any way. Keep a distance so that they behave naturally.
Supplies to take: Drinking water, headlamp with extra batteries, and a blacklight

LOOK UP
Do you see Scorpius, the constellation due south? The red star Antares is considered the heart of the scorpion.

Scorpions feed primarily on insects.

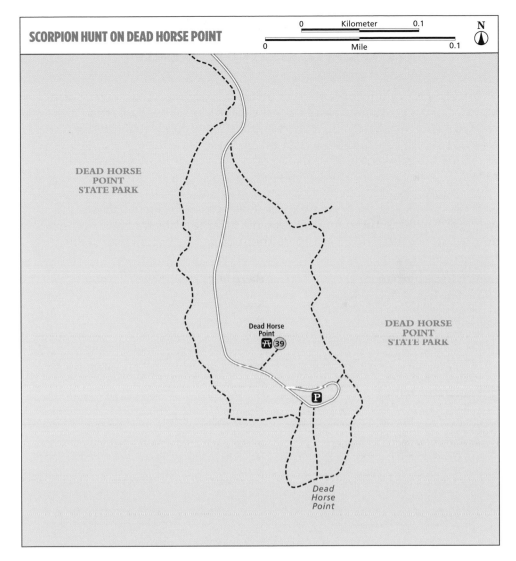

DEAD HORSE
POINT
STATE PARK

Dead Horse
Point

DEAD HORSE
POINT
STATE PARK

Dead
Horse
Point

FINDING THE TRAILHEAD

From Moab follow US 191 north to the junction with UT 313. Turn left and follow UT 313 to the top of the mesa. As you reach the top, don't miss the left turn to stay on UT 313. Follow UT 313 to the Dead Horse Point. The picnic area will be on the left before the loop parking lot at the end of the road.

Dead Horse Point picnic area GPS: N38 29.227' / W109 44.411'

THE ADVENTURE

Pull out your blacklight and begin your hunt. The rock outcroppings throughout the picnic area provide a wonderful opportunity to look for scorpions. Also check under the low shrubs within the picnic area. Once you spot one, step back a little and watch it for a while. If you're lucky and patient, you may get to see one grab an insect. Once you've found your first scorpion, you will never forget the experience.

40. ASTROPHOTOGRAPHY ON DEAD HORSE POINT

One of the most photographed spots in the greater Moab area, Dead Horse Point provides a beautiful view of the gooseneck in the Colorado River. Photographing it at night with the Milky Way across the sky takes your photos to a whole other level.

Activity: Astrophotography
Adventure rating: 1
Start: Dead Horse Point parking area
Distance: 0.1 mile out and back
Elevation loss: 21 feet
Difficulty: Easy
Trip time: 1–6 hours, depending on time-lapse versus still shots
Best seasons: Any season
Timing: About 1 hour after sunset
Dog-friendly: Yes, must be on 6-foot leash and under control
Trail surface: Concrete and asphalt
Fees and permits: $$
Contact: Dead Horse Point State Park visitor center, (435) 259-2614

Land status: State park
Nearest town: Moab
Other area users: Hikers, sightseers
Maps: https://stateparks.utah.gov/parks/dead-horse/map/
Special considerations: The park closes at 10 p.m. for day-use visitation. During the summer months, you will need to camp to complete this adventure.
Other: Be mindful as you move through this rugged landscape. A misstep can result in injury.
Supplies to take: Drinking water, headlamp with extra batteries, camera equipment, and tripod

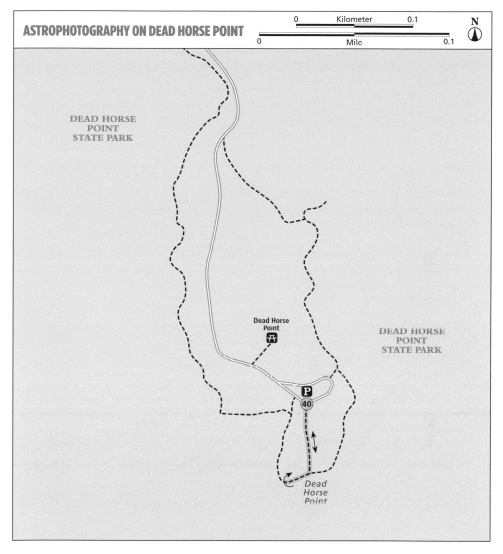

DEAD HORSE
POINT
STATE PARK

Dead Horse
Point

DEAD HORSE
POINT
STATE PARK

Dead
Horse
Point

FINDING THE TRAILHEAD

From Moab follow US 191 north to the junction with UT 313. Turn left and follow UT 313 to the top of the mesa. As you reach the top, don't miss the left turn to stay on UT 313. Follow UT 313 to the Dead Horse Point at the end of the road.
Dead Horse Point GPS: N38 28.147' / W109 44.397'

Other Opportunities to Enjoy the Night Sky
PARK RANGER–LED EVENTS
During summer, the park offers star parties. These evening events highlight the night sky found within the park and offer the opportunity to look through a telescope at deep space objects such as nebulae, galaxies, star clusters, and more. For more information on the timing of these events, visit https:// stateparks.utah.gov/parks/dead-horse/events/.

THE ADVENTURE

The viewing platform on Dead Horse Point give you a high vantage point for photographing the gooseneck. Timing your visit for midsummer will give you the core of the Milky Way Galaxy over the gooseneck. Try a few different places around the Point for something unique.

GLOSSARY

abandoned meander: a former stream channel that was cut off from the rest of the river

alcove: a recess in a cliff wall

alkaline: having a pH of greater than 7

amphitheater: a circular feature in a hillside

anticline: a ridge-shaped fold of stratified rock in which the strata slope downward from the crest

arch: a semi-curved opening in a rock created by weathering

archaeoastronomy: the study of indigenous understanding of and connection with astronomy

asphyxiate: kill by depriving of air

astrophotography: photography of night sky

basalt flow: a pathway where molten lava flowed

biological soil crust: a living soil crust made of cyanobacteria, algae, fungus, moss, and lichen in symbiosis

bioluminescence: the biochemical emission of light by a living creature

Bortle scale: a scale to measure light pollution's impact on the night sky

butte: an isolated hill with steep sides

capstone: a stone fixed on top of something

celestial: relating to the sky

constellation: a group of stars forming a recognizable figure

crinoid: a type of echinoderm sea life

derrick: a framework over an oil well

electrolyte: an ionized constituent of a living cell

ecliptic: the path the sun, moon, and planets follow across the sky

entrenched: firmly established and difficult to change

equinox: a day when day and night are equal length

erratic: unpredictable or irregular

exoplanet: a planet around another star

flash flood: a sudden flood due to rain

fossil fuel: a natural fuel created by past living organisms

galaxy: a system of millions or billions of stars together with gas and dust held together by the gravity of a black hole

granary: a storage house for grains

gravity: the force that attracts bodies of mass toward each other

habituated: become accustomed to

hoodoo: a column of weathered rock

indigenous: occurring naturally in a particular place

kelvin: the SI base unit of thermodynamic temperatures

laccolith: a mass of igneous rock that forms a dome

LED: light-emitting diode

lux: the SI unit of illuminance, equal to one lumen per square meter

magnitude: a numerical code for star brightness

megafauna: large mammals of the ice age era

mesa: a wide and long area of land with steep sides

metamorphic: marked by metamorphosis

meteor: dust, ice, or rock that exists in space

monocline: a large, upright block of rock

monsoon: a rainy season following a monsoon wind

natural bridge: a natural bridge across a canyon created by flowing water

nebula: a cloud of gas and dust in space

nuclear fusion: the fusion of hydrogen atoms into helium atoms

nyctophile: a lover of the night

petroglyph: a pecked symbol in rock

pictograph: a painted symbol on rock

planet: a celestial body orbiting the sun

planetary nebula: the shell of a low-mass star lost to space at the end of the star's life

Rayleigh scattering: the scattering of light by particulates in the atmosphere

saline: salty in nature

sedimentary: rock formed by sediment placed by water or wind

skyglow: the glow of artificial light above communities

slot canyon: a narrow canyon with high walls

solstice: the longest or shortest day of the year due to the sun reaching maximum or minimum declination

spire: a long, tapering rock

stalagmite: a tapered structure rising from the floor of a cave

stalagtite: a tapered structure hanging from the roof of a cave

star: a celestial body that creates its own light by nuclear fusion

star cluster: a cluster of stars

steppe: a large area of flat landscape

superstition: an excessive credulous belief for supernatural beings

terrestrial: relating to earth

torpor: a state of mental or physical inactivity

universe: all matter and space considered as a whole

UV ray: ultraviolet ray

wag bag: a bag used to carry human waste

zenith: the point directly above

zodiacal light: a faint, elongated triangle of light stretching from the horizon along the ecliptic

REFERENCES

"**Mechanistic, ecological, and evolutionary consequences of artificial light at night for insects: review and prospective**," Emmanuel Desouhant*, Elisa Gomes, Nathalie Mondy, and Isabelle Amat UMR 5558, Laboratoire de Biom etrie et Biologie Evolutive, CNRS, Universite Claude Bernard Lyon 1, F-69622 Villeurbanne, France, and UMR5023 LEHNA, ENTPE, CNRS, Universite Claude Bernard Lyon 1, F-69622 Villeurbanne, France.

"**Dose-dependent responses of avian daily rhythms to artificial light at night**," Maaike de Jong, Lizanne Jeninga, Jenny Q. Ouyang, Kees van Oers, Kamiel Spoelstra, Marcel E.Visser.

"**Individual-based measurements of light intensity provide new insights into the effects of artificial light at night on daily rhythms of urban-dwelling songbirds**," Davide M. Dominoni, Esther O. Carmona-Wagner, Michaela Hofmann, Bart Kranstauber, and Jesko Partecke.

"**Ecological effects of artificial light at night on wild plants**," Jonathan Bennie*, Thomas W. Davies, David Cruse, and Kevin J. Gaston. Environment and Sustainability Institute, University of Exeter, Penryn Campus, Penryn TR10 9FE, UK.

Report 4 of the Council on Science and Public Health (A-12) American Medical Association: "Light Pollution: Adverse Health Effects of Nighttime Lighting," David Blask, PhD, MD (Tulane University School of Medicine); George Brainard, PhD (Jefferson Medical College); Ronald Gibbons, PhD (Virginia Tech); Steven Lockley, PhD (Brigham and Women's Hospital, Harvard Medical School); Richard Stevens, PhD (University Connecticut Health Center); and Mario Motta, MD (CSAPH, Tufts Medical School).

"**Evaluating the Association between Artificial Light-at-Night Exposure and Breast and Prostate Cancer Risk in Spain (MCC-Spain Study)**," Ariadna Garcia-Saenz, Alejandro Sánchez de Miguel, Ana Espinosa, Antonia Valentin, Núria Aragonés, Javier Llorca, Pilar Amiano, Vicente Martín Sánchez, Marcela Guevara, Rocío Capelo, Adonina Tardón, Rosana Peiró-Perez, José Juan Jiménez-Moleón, Aina Roca-Barceló, Beatriz Pérez-Gómez, Trinidad Dierssen-Sotos, Tania Fernández-Villa, Conchi Moreno-Iribas, Victor Moreno, Javier García-Pérez, Gemma Castaño-Vinyals, Marina Pollán, Martin Aubé, and Manolis Kogevinas.

"Light at night increases body mass by shifting the time of food intake," Laura K. Fonken, Joanna L. Workman, James C. Walton, Zachary M. Weil, John S. Morris, Abraham Haim, and Randy J. Nelson. Departments of Neuroscience and Psychology, Ohio State University, Columbus, OH 43210; and Israeli Center for Interdisciplinary Research in Chronobiology, University of Haifa, Haifa 31905, Israel.

ADDITIONAL READING

Outfit your mind for every element of your starry sky adventures and keep exploring with these FalconGuides:

Hiking Utah: A Guide to Utah's Greatest Hiking Adventures by Bill and Russ Schneider
Hiking Zion and Bryce Canyon National Parks: A Guide to Southwestern Utah's Greatest Hikes by Erik Molvar
Hiking Canyonlands and Arches National Parks: A Guide to More Than 60 Great Hikes by Bill Schneider
Camping Utah: A Comprehensive Guide to Public Tent and RV Campgrounds by Donna Ikenberry
Desert Hiking Tips: Expert Advice on Desert Hiking and Driving by Bruce Grubbs
Night Sky: A Falcon Field Guide by Nicholas Nigro